Document Style Guide

for Architectural, Engineering, Environmental, and Construction Firms

by
LORI JO OSWALD, PH.D.
Wordsworth LLC

WORDSWORTH

Writing, Editing, & Document Formatting Svcs.

Words worth writing are ... words worth writing well.
Wordsworth ...
because your words are worth it.

TIPS FOR USING

Thank you for purchasing Wordsworth LLC's Style Guide for professional firms. This has been designed specifically for architectural, engineering, environmental, and construction companies and their contractors but may be useful to other professional firms as well as individual writers.

This can be a useful training tool. The first six chapters can be assigned to personnel to read (it may take 2 to 3 hours); the rest can be used for reference on an as-needed basis.

If you would like to order a Microsoft Word version of this document to personalize it for your company, just order from our Web sites, either wordsworthwriting.net or formsinword.com. You may wish to substitute (or add to) your own acronym list, your own references style, your own font style, or your own sample documents. There are sections that are "rules" that should stay the same, and then there is a section titled Company Style, which can be changed.

I would like this to be a document that makes your job easier as well as makes the company look better, so your input is welcome and encouraged. If you have any questions or suggestions related to this style guide, I will be glad to answer them at no extra charge. Just e-mail your questions to us at editor@wordsworthwriting.net.

Our documents tell our clients a lot about us, and they should be error-free; it is therefore essential that you allow time for every document to be reviewed before it goes out. Thank you for caring about your company's words, style, and presentation!

Sincerely,
Lori Jo Oswald, Ph.D., Author
Owner, Wordsworth LLC

ACKNOWLEDGMENTS

I am grateful to the many technical editing clients I have worked with over the last 20 years.

For sources, I have used and highly recommend *Merriam-Webster's Collegiate Dictionary* and the *Chicago Manual of Style*. There are many other excellent references out there, but these are my two favorites.

Thank you to Eva Nagy, my assistant editor, for her suggestions on this document.

TABLE OF CONTENTS

LIST OF TABLES AND FIGURES

TABLES

FIGURES

1.0   INTRODUCTION

The purpose of this style guide is to provide writing tips, editing guidelines, and samples for your company. But this style guide has other functions as well. I have included specific acronym and style lists to help make report writing and editing at your company easier.

Consider this a guide in helping you through the writing or editing process. It is subject to change, and you are encouraged to add your suggestions and changes and give them to the technical editor for inclusion in future versions of this document.

Another element of this guide, and one which you might find slightly confusing, is that I have written it so that it not only guides you but also can *become* your own company style guide. (A Microsoft Word version can be purchased online at wordsworthwriting.net or formsinword.com if you wish to have it in Word for ease of adding your company's name and other personalizing touches.)

Why is a style guide important? The answers are consistency, clarity, and professionalism. Every document—e-mail, memo, letter, proposal, or report—gives an impression to clients or prospective clients about our company. As one editor said, "What we sell are reports." One mistake, such as writing 2.5 liters instead of .25 liters, can have serious consequences as well as make us seem unprofessional. Errors distract from messages, cause credibility problems, and can communicate the wrong information. Our clients expect and demand high-quality writing.

Do we expect you to catch every error or check for every possible item mentioned in this guide? Definitely not—this is mostly a reference manual and will mainly be used by the technical editor. There is no such thing as a perfect draft. The writer handles the prewriting and writing stages, while the technical editor edits and proofreads the document. Peer reviewers can also serve as helpful editors. This guide has sections for both writers and editors.

Editing and writing are different tasks and require different people to do them. All good writers have editors. When an editor makes changes, corrections, and suggestions on a copy, there is nothing personal intended toward the writer. This is simply a common—and important—

step in creating a strong, clear, and clean document.

Please don't let fear of your high school English teacher's red pen prevent you from passing on your company documentation to an editor. The editor does not judge you personally, talk about you, or think you are less of a person because your document has mistakes.

I will tell you an editor's secret: We love mistakes. We love finding and fixing them. We love thinking about words and the best ways they can be used to accomplish the assigned task. Additionally, a document with mistakes in it is much more interesting to read than a near-perfect one. And never once, in nearly 30 years of editing, have I thought poorly of an author because of the document I was reading. I think only of the words themselves, the purpose of the document as a whole, and the intended audience.

Most important is that the writer—and the company in general—knows that each document—no matter how small—should go through a review process, including the technical editor and at least one peer. Reviewers need to edit for the following:

- Grammar, punctuation, and spelling
- Style and format
- Organization and logical presentation
- Readability and appropriateness to the intended audience
- Inclusion of all required elements (i.e., Executive Summary, List of Acronyms and Abbreviations, References, etc.)
- Consistency and accuracy of data in the text, figures, and tables
- Figures, Tables, and References (text locations and consistent format)

There are many resources to help with writing and editing, in addition to this guide. An English handbook, such as those required in college English classes, is useful. I also rely on *Merriam-Webster's New Collegiate Dictionary* for final decisions about spelling, capitalization, and hyphenation. Another important source for editors, and for some of the information in this style guide, is the *Chicago Manual of Style*. It is an excellent, detailed manual that you should add to your library.

2.0   DOCUMENT REVIEW POLICY

As part of your company's commitment to quality control, all documents should go through the following review process (this may be different at your company):

- The initial document (or revision) is prepared by at least one employee, who then sends it to the technical editor.

- The author then submits the document to one or more qualified peers or supervisors. The reviewer keeps track changes on so that the author and technical editor can review those changes.

- The peer reviewer sends the document back to the author for revisions.

- The document is reviewed by a technical editor, who edits for grammar, content, organization, style, and formatting.

- The editor's changes are reviewed by the author. Track changes are accepted and comments are addressed and deleted, unless the author wants the peer reviewer to see them. Track changes for new sections or author changes are turned back on, so the editor can review these changes in the final version.

- The final version is e-mailed back to the technical editor who checks the changes by the author and peer reviewer and submits the document back to the author.

- The document is approved by a senior manager.

Since writing and editing are different processes requiring different skills, it is strongly recommended that all document writers obtain at least one edit from someone else.

Even formal letters and memos should be reviewed by someone other than the author. Proposals, letter reports, and draft and final reports should all be read—at a minimum—by a peer reviewer, a technical editor, and a senior reviewer.

Figure 2-1 shows the editing review process I recommend. Of course, not all companies can afford this complete process every time, but I hope if I convince you of nothing else in this manual, it is that a technical editor is an essential element in quality control. Your company will be presented to your clients as more professional, and you will reduce or eliminate risk in making embarrassing mistakes (often I have found inaccuracies in table or figure data and the text, for example).

All writers, including editors who write manuals, need an editor.

Figure 2-1   Document Review Flowchart

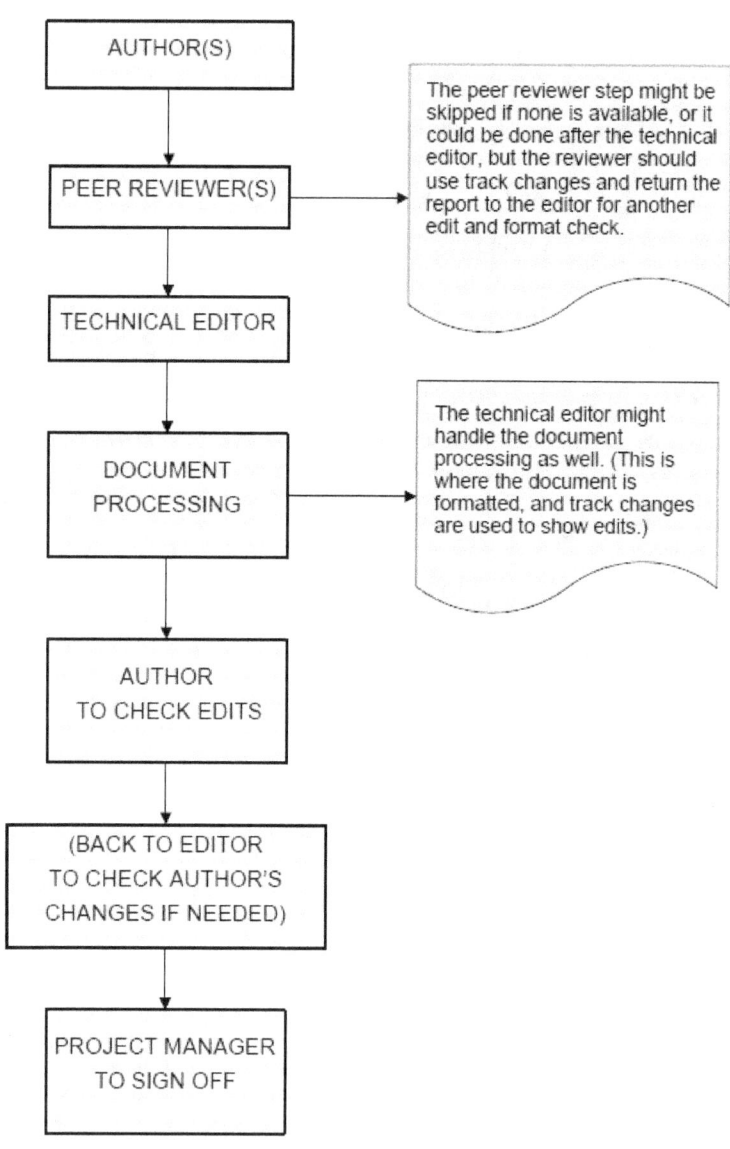

2.1 Peer Review

Peer and senior edits are made to evaluate the concepts and conclusions from a technical standpoint, as well as to provide any other feedback as needed. Remember, the more readers your document has before it goes to the client, the better!

2.2 Technical Editing

The technical editor, or someone else qualified to edit the report, should edit the document in the following areas:

- Evaluating grammar, punctuation, spelling, house style, and format (using this style guide as a source);

- Checking the organization of sections within the document, as well as the overall document;

- Looking for conciseness and readability;

- Making sure there is consistency among and within the text, tables, and figures;

- Determining whether there is a logical and clear progression from findings to conclusions; and

- Looking for the presence in the text of all the required sections.

Here are some specific areas the technical editor should check for in each document:

- Figures, graphs, and tables are clear;

- Data in text match data in tables, numbers in tables and figures are correct;

- Figures and tables are referred to in the text; figures and tables either directly follow the first textual reference, or are located on the next page following the first textual reference;

- An acronym (and abbreviation) list is included;

- Each acronym is defined the first time (and only the first time) it is used in the regular text (exceptions: Transmittal Letter, Executive Summary, figures and tables, and resumes are treated as separate documents);

- The use and capitalization of acronyms are correct (per the acronym list in this style guide);

- Font size and style are correct;

- References are in proper company format;

- Bullets are used instead of numbers with lists, unless numbers represent sequential steps;

- The use of *and/or* is avoided if possible;

- Appendices are referenced in order in the text and are complete;

- Maps are clear, legible, and checked for spelling;

- The text is not too technical-sounding or filled with jargon or vague phrases;

- Title page has proper elements, including the client's name and address, project number, and date;

- Table of Contents matches text, including page numbering, headings, appendices, and titles of tables and figures;

- Transmittal letter and executive summary are edited;

- The headings are worded properly to reflect the text that follows;

- There are enough headings; and

- The numbering and font styles of the headings are appropriate.

It is also important that the technical editor, the original writer, or a peer check the document after it is returned from document processing to be sure all changes were made correctly and that the formatting is still correct.

Try to understand the time needed by the technical editor to do a thorough edit. Although many reports require little editing (rewriting) but instead require mostly proofreading (fixing errors in grammar, punctuation, and style), the average time involved in technical editing is six pages per hour, which means a medium-length report will require at least 6 to 12 hours to complete. Figures and tables often add more time. Also, remember that the editor probably has other documents to complete before yours. Try not to say, "Just do a quick edit," to the editor. There is no good way to do that. You would be asking for a shoddy, incomplete job.

2.3   Document Processing (or Formatting)

The document processor puts the document in the proper format (i.e., report, proposal, letter, memo) using the appropriate fonts, margins, headings, footings, etc., according to the specifications in this style guide, unless other specifications are given by the author or technical editor.

The document processor also does the following:

- Adds the Table of Contents page
- Inserts tables and figures and the correctly formatted table and figure headings (using the "Captions" feature in Microsoft Word)
- Inserts page breaks
- Inserts page numbers

Nowadays, the technical editor often performs the Document Processing duties since documents are usually edited in Microsoft Word, on a computer. Some editors still prefer to mark up the hard copy; this can allow for a more careful, if slower, read, and if the company affords it and the editor prefers it, wonderful! Most of my clients are rushed, especially regarding proposals, and I am expected to do it all and quickly.

3.0 PUNCTUATION ("THE RULES")

This section lists common punctuation rules and errors with examples similar to the ones we encounter in your company's documents.

3.1 Apostrophes

- Apostrophes are not used for plural forms of years and acronyms: 1990s, USTs.

- Apostrophes are used to show possession. The apostrophe precedes the "s" when the noun is singular; it follows the "s" when the noun is plural. There is no need for a second "s" after the apostrophe. Examples: the client's bill, the USEPA's decision, Robert Edwards' letter, your company's documents.

- Its and it's are often confused; *its* is the possessive form, and *it's* is a contraction for *it is*. Examples: The agency believed its decision was correct. It's not important to me. (Do not use it's in technical writing; see next bullet item.)

- Do not use contractions: it's, can't, don't, won't, wouldn't, etc.

3.2 Capitalization

- Generally, we tend to use capitals unnecessarily. If you are not sure, you probably do not need to capitalize the word. To be sure, you can use *Merriam-Webster's New Collegiate Dictionary*; if it is capitalized there, go ahead and capitalize it. Also, follow the guidelines in this section.

- Acronyms and abbreviations are usually in all capital letters, although the words they are based on are often not capitalized. To be sure, check the abbreviations and acronyms list in Section 13.0 of this style guide. Example: inside diameter variation (IDV).

- Capitalize titles only when they directly precede a person's name or are part of an address: The source of the information was Project Manager Jane Szmanski. The project manager is Jane Szmanski. Jane Szmanski, project manager, is. . . .

- Generally, capitalize counties, states, municipalities, cities, and boroughs when they are part of a name. They are usually lowercased when they precede a name: Kansas City, the Municipality of Anchorage, the state of Alaska, the city of Palmer, Washington State, the Pacific Northwest (the proper name of a region), northern Washington (a general direction).

- If you are referring to a specific document, table, entity, or organization, capitalize it. If not, lowercase: draft reports, *Draft Report 1 for Bethel Landfill*, Figure 1-5; the figure; the Environmental Services Agency; the agency; the Federal Bureau of Standards; federal, state, municipal, and city agencies; the federal Department of Transportation; the federal government; Congress and the Senate; the state senate and the state legislature; the department; the Department of Public Works.

- Do not capitalize "the" before a company or institution name: the University of Alaska Anchorage.

- Capitalize the first word in columns and bullet lists if each item is a complete sentence or is particularly lengthy. For simple words or short phrases that finish the sentence preceding the bullet list, lowercase the individual bullet items, use commas or semicolons at the end of each item as is appropriate, and end the final list item with a period. For example:

  The ground is

  - hard,

  - cold, and

  - dark.

- Capitalize specific geographic names but not general terms: John, Paul, and Mary creeks, Yukon River, the lakes, Lake Ontario, lakes Stephan and Willamette, Winston Lake.

3.3   Colons

- Colons are often used to precede lists. They are also used to precede clauses or phrases that clarify or illustrate.

- Use only one space after a colon (and after a semicolon, for that matter). The contractor discovered three flaws: first, a loose bolt; second, a missing nut; and third, a broken screw.

- Colons in text are used after complete sentences (i.e., you should be able to replace the colon with a period). The same rule should apply to colons before bullet lists (but we are flexible here and allow for an incomplete sentence before a bullet list if necessary). Examples: We have six requests: the first . . . , the second . . . , etc. Bring four items to the campsite: food, bedding, equipment, and bear spray.

- In the text, do not use a colon after the word "includes" or "including" unless the words "the following" appear after. Example: The punctuation list includes commas, semicolons, and periods. The list includes the following: cheese, bread, and water. It is acceptable to use a colon after "includes" or "including" before a bullet list, but it is still preferable to have a complete sentence before any colon.

- Although you usually need a complete sentence before a colon, you do not need one after a colon. However, it is not wrong to have a complete sentence after a colon. Examples: I have six pets: two dogs, two cats, and two horses. The monitoring well data were incomplete: additional testing was required. (Note: The writer could have used a semicolon, a period, or a comma with a conjunction [and] instead of a colon in the last sentence.)

- Use a colon after a salutation in a letter instead of a comma (Dear Mr. Jones:).

- A colon can be used after one word, as we have been using throughout this document with the word "Example." Example: This is such a case. For example: Here is another one.

- When the expressions namely, for instance, for example, or that is are used in a sentence to introduce a list, a comma is usually used instead of a colon. Example: Birch's study included the three most critical areas, namely, McBurney Point, Rockland, and Effingham.

3.4   Commas

Comma rules can be confusing, so we have provided subheadings for each use to help you find the appropriate rule quickly.

3.4.1 Using Commas in a Series

Always use a comma before "and" or "or" in a series of three or more items. This is a style requirement, not a rule. You might notice that most newspapers use Associated Press (AP) style, which does not use the last comma in a series. Most magazines use the *Chicago Manual of Style*, which does require it. It is standard in formal writing to use the comma. For example:

- Mammals in Area A include caribou, fox, and lemmings; mammals in Area B include polar bear, walrus, and several species of whales and seals.

- It was a fast, simple, and inexpensive process.

Incorrect in Technical Writing: The corporation requires its employees to be loyal, hard working and prepared.

Correction: The corporation requires its employees to be loyal, hard working, and prepared.

When adjectives modifying the same noun can be reversed and make sense, or when they can be separated by either "and" or "or," they should be separated by commas:

- The drawing was of a modern, sleek, swept-wing airplane.

But when an adjective modifies a phrase, no comma is needed, as in the following example, where *damaged* modifies *radar beacon system*.

- The company investigated the damaged radar beacon system.

If there are only two items in a series, no comma is necessary.

- The drawing was of a modern sleek airplane.

3.4.2 Using Commas to Separate Complete Sentences

If you have two independent clauses (i.e., complete sentences that could stand on their own) separated by a coordinating conjunction (and, but, for, or, so, yet), put a comma before the coordinating conjunction. If the second clause is not an independent clause, do not use the comma before the coordinating conjunction.

- The pack ice breaks off from shore ice in June, and the shore is free of ice from late July until mid-August.

- The Gubik formation is mainly of marine origin and consists of lenses of gravel, sand, silt, and clay.

3.4.3 Using Commas to Set off Phrases (Which, That, Who)

Usually, when you use the relative pronoun "which," you have a phrase that needs to be set off from the rest of the sentence with two commas. Usually when "that" is used, there are no commas. Whether or not to use commas before and after a clause beginning with "who" depends on the meaning of the sentence. If the information following the word "who" is essential to the meaning of the sentence, do not use commas; if it can be eliminated without changing the meaning of the sentence, do use commas.

- The company's new style guide, which will be in use by December 1, ensures consistency in all documents.

- The style guide that the company is presently using is outdated.

- The editor, who studied at the University of Washington, is based in the Fresno office.

- The editor who is the most skilled in that area is in the Palmer office.

3.4.4 Using Commas with Names, Titles, and Addresses

Commas are used to separate distinct items in the text. Therefore, if you write an address on one line, separate the elements in this way: Chris Polsky, 4117 Ravensdale Road, Seattle, Washington. Note that the state is spelled out in the text, but in letters and addresses, use the postal code abbreviation (listed in Section 13.0, Abbreviations and Acronyms):

> Chris Polsky
> 4117 Ravensdale Road
> Seattle, WA 97506
> (206) 777-7677
>
> Dear Chris Polsky:

Note that in the salutation, above, a colon is used instead of a comma in formal writing. Also, I addressed "Chris Polsky" instead of "Mr." or "Ms." Polsky because I am not sure whether Chris is a man or a woman, based on the name.

Here are some additional uses of commas with names, titles, and addresses:

- Toronto, Ontario, Canada

- Sally Jo Rogers, Ph.D.

- John Smith, P.E.

- LMB, Inc.

3.4.5   Using Commas in Numbers

Use a comma in numbers larger than 999: 131,000, 9,000, 800.

3.4.6   Using Commas after Introductory Phrases

In technical writing, always use a comma after an introductory phrase, in order to avoid confusion. For example, notice how the comma clarifies this confusing sentence: To be successful managers with MBAs must continue to learn. Revised: To be successful, managers with MBAs must continue to learn.

3.4.7   Using Commas with Quotation Marks

Commas and periods always go inside the closing quotation marks; semicolons and colons always go outside closing quotation marks.

- Smith said, "I didn't do it," after he saw me.

- I said, "Yes, you did."

- I don't know why he said he "didn't"; it was clear that he did.

3.4.8   Using Commas in Dates

- August 27, 1999, was the day he proposed.

- The subcontractor conducted the site assessment in June 1998.

3.5   Dangling and Misplaced Modifiers

Dangling modifiers can be tricky to spot, but the rewards are worth it. A dangling modifier is a word or phrase that modifies a word which does not appear in the sentence (or is in the wrong part of a sentence). Here are some examples (the first two are from grammar.about.com):

- Sipping cocktails on the balcony, the moon looked magnificent. (This sounds like the moon drinks.)

- Exhausted after the long hike, the shady hammock was a welcome sight. (How can a hammock be exhausted?)

- After looking behind the garbage container, the polar bear was located.

Spotting these can be challenging, but fixing them is easy. Add in the subject. For the third bullet item above, for example, add the missing subject after the comma: After looking behind the garbage container, the scientist found the polar bear.

Here are some more humorous examples from eddiesnipes.com:

- While reading the newspaper, the cat jumped on the table.

- The young girl was walking the dog in a short skirt.

- The dog was chasing the boy with the spiked collar.

- The hunter crouched behind a tree waiting for a bear to come along with a bow and arrow.

- The woman walked the dog in purple suede cowboy boots.

- We saw dinosaurs on a field trip to the natural history museum.

- Hopping briskly through the vegetable garden, I saw a toad.

3.6   Dashes

Dashes come in three lengths: hyphens (-) (which are discussed in Section 3.9), en dashes (–), and em dashes (—).

3.6.1   En Dashes

- Our company's style is generally to have one space around en dashes. En dashes are the shorter dash.

- Microsoft Word will automatically change a hyphen to an en dash as you type, as long as you have the space before and after the hyphen.

3.6.2 *Em Dashes*

- Dashes are usually used to emphasize the text in between them—to tell the reader this is important and look here—so they should be used sparingly.

- Dashes can also be used to define words. Anorexia nervosa—an eating disorder characterized by an aversion to eating and an obsession with losing weight—is common among young female gymnasts and ballet dancers.

- Type two hyphens with no spaces around them, and Microsoft Word should automatically replace them with a dash.

- There are no spaces around em dashes.

3.7 Ellipses

Ellipsis points (plural: ellipses) are a set of three or four spaced dots (periods on the keyboard) showing missing text from quotations. Usually you can quote without having to resort to using them (as in the first example below), but here are some ways they are used.

- Example without ellipsis: Peter Singer said that stones "do not have interests" because they can't suffer, while a mouse does have "an interest in not being kicked down the road, because it will suffer if it is" (1975).

- Quotation with ellipsis: Yi-Fu Taun, author *of Dominance and Affection: The Making of Pets*, said that the breeding process is used to make animals more useful or desirable for humans: "With the horse . . . humans have tried to make the animal both larger and smaller" (1984).

- Use a fourth "dot"—a sentence-ending period—along with the ellipsis points when an ellipsis comes at the end of your sentence or when the material you have deleted contains at least one period: Summer also said that people have described personal space as "a small shell, a soap bubble, an aura. . . ." In *Animal Liberation*, Peter Singer wrote, "Nearly all the external signs which lead us to infer pain in other humans can be seen in other species. . . . Behavioral signs—writhing, facial contortions, moaning, yelping or other forms of calling, attempts to avoid the source of pain, appearance of fear at the prospect of its repetition, and so on—are present" (1975).

- Note spacing requirements: with three "dots," space before and after each one; with four dots, do not space before the first one (or after the last one if a quotation mark immediately follows it).

- The ellipsis points should not be separated at the end of a line and into the following line. This can be a problem in right-justified text. You may have to revise your sentence to fix it.

3.8   Exclamation Points

- Avoid! Avoid! Avoid! They do not belong in formal writing! In fact, most good writers don't use them at all, except perhaps in a quotation! (Jane screamed, "Eeek!") And especially never use more than one!! That would be most inappropriate!!!!!!!

3.9   Hyphenation

- Hyphens connect related items, often modifiers that precede a noun (tie-in, toll-free call, two-thirds, one-year-old child).

- Hyphens are often used unnecessarily after prefixes. Check the lists in *Merriam-Webster's New Collegiate Dictionary* if in doubt. (To save time, nowadays I go to www.m-w.com and just type in the words I need to check there.)

- Here are some examples of words that do *not* take hyphens after the prefixes: preexisting, semivolatile, nonprofit, nonhazardous, nonnegotiable. See Table 3-1 for a list of prefixes that do not usually take a hyphen (always confirm at www.m-w.com or in your Merriam-Webster's dictionary if you can).

- For the examples in which *Chicago Manual of Style* does not take a hyphen but Merriam-Webster's does (e.g., coworker or co-worker and prolife or pro-life), I usually go with Merriam-Webster's dictionary. It is my "go-to" source for capitalization, hyphens, and spelling. I have included, in this manual, a list of commonly used (and confused) words; I use them exactly as in that list.

Table 3-1   Prefixes Not Requiring Hyphens

Prefix	Example	Exception
after	aftereffect	
anti	antisocial	
bi	bilingual	

Prefix	Example	Exception
co	coworker	*Note: Merriam-Webster's does use a hyphen with most co- words.*
counter	counterbalance	
equi	equilibrium	
extra	extracurricular	
infra	infrared	
inter	interstimulus	
intra	intraspecific	
macro	macrocosm	
mega	megawatt	
meta	metacognitive	meta-analysis
micro	microorganism	
mid	midterm	
mini	minisession	
multi	multiphase	
non	nonsignificant	non-achievement-oriented students
over	overaggressive	
post	posttest	*I know it looks like "post" should take a hyphen, but check the list in Webster's (or m-w.com); it rarely does. Still, if a company insists or its style guide demands, I will not argue, and I will use the hyphen.*
pre	preexperimental	pre-1970, pre-UAA trial
pro	prowar	*Note: Merriam-Webster's does use hyphens with most "pro-" words.*
pseudo	pseudoscience	
re	reevaluate	re-pair (pair again), re-form (form again)
semi	semidarkness	
socio	socioeconomic	
sub	subtest	
super	superordinate	
supra	supraliminal	
ultra	ultrahigh	
un	unbiased	un-ionized (not ionized)
under	underdeveloped	

Source: *Chicago Manual of Style*

- Exceptions to the above include the following: if the prefix stands alone (pre- and postclosure elements), if the root word is capitalized (mid-August, non-American), if the root is a number (pre-1900), if the resulting word can have two meanings (retreat and re-treat or un-ionized and unionized), or if the second element consists of more than one word (non-English-speaking, non-achievement-oriented students).

- Generally, hyphenate words with the prefixes ex, all, and self and the suffix elect: all-encompassing, self-employed, president-elect.

- Hyphenate a numeral and a unit of measure used as an adjective: three 1,000-gallon tanks; 3-, 4-, and 6-inch-diameter pipes.

- Do not use a hyphen after adverbs ending in –ly: previously installed wells.

- Do not hyphenate Latin terms: in situ (per Webster's; you will see this term handled differently by different companies and agencies however, so if a client prefers another way— hyphenated or italicized or both—go ahead and use that style for that client.

- Hyphenate two words of equal value used as modifiers: gray-brown soil.

- Hyphenate compound modifiers when one word modifies or defines another but does not separately define the noun being referred to: dark-green building (but no hyphen in large green building, since large does not modify green).

- Before a noun, hyphenate a compound consisting of a noun and a participle: decision-making skills, broad-based experience. But do not hyphenate if the expression follows the noun: Her experience is broad based. The well is 73 feet deep.

- Hyphenate a phrase used as an adjective before a noun (up-to-date account) but not if it follows the noun (the account was up to date).

- Hyphenate compounds containing numbers that precede the noun: 23-year-old woman, twentieth-century innovation, one-year program, 7-foot depth, 7-foot-wide opening. But there is no hyphen in the following: in three years, 35 gallons of fuel, the woman was 23 years old.

- Hyphenate fractions that are spelled out: one-half, two-thirds.

- Hyphenate when referring to specific figures and tables: Figure 4-1, Table 3-7.

- Although most of the time numerals 10 and over are not spelled out, if you must begin a sentence with a compound number, do spell out and use a hyphen: forty-six, one hundred sixty-three.

3.10   Parentheses and Brackets

Generally, try not to overuse parentheses. Some editors believe that if it is not important enough to include as part of the text, then delete it. If it is important, set it off with commas or dashes instead. But, of course, sometimes it is necessary or useful to include parenthetical expressions. So here are some tips to guide you:

- Periods go inside parentheses when a complete sentence is contained within the parentheses. (We have tentatively scheduled this meeting for June 16, 2001.) Otherwise, put the period outside the parentheses: Previous studies found the landfill area safe (Compton, 1989).

- No other punctuation mark should directly precede the first parenthesis mark. The findings were explained by Smith (1989), and they were confirmed by Jones (1993).

- Within a parenthetical phrase, if you have another parenthetical phase, use brackets: Buck (in *The Call of the Wild* [1903] by Jack London) was one of the most developed dog characters in literature.

- However, for code regulations that already contain parentheses, use brackets on the outside where you would normally use parentheses: [24 CFR 1600(4)(5)].

3.11   Quotation Marks

- Quotation marks are used only around direct quotes (i.e., words taken from a source exactly as they were written). If you are changing or condensing the information from another source, still give credit, but do not use quotation marks. The latter is an indirect quote.

- _Direct Quote, Complete Sentence_: John Smith said, "This is wrong."

- _Direct Quote, Word or Phrase Only_: Darrell Cohen said he is "positive" the actions were appropriate.

- _Direct Quote, Word or Phrases with Material Deleted_: According to Daniel Danielson, the site was "always empty . . . and left alone."

- _Direct Quote, Complete Except Material Deleted from End of Sentence_: Patricia Meyers said, "I don't think I can agree with that assessment. . . ."

- _Direct Quote, Material Missing from Beginning of Quoted Sentence_: Hillary Capra said that the area "is in need of a bulldozer and explosives." (Note: There are no ellipses marks used at the beginning of a partial quotation; the word "that" preceding the quote as well as the lower case "is" tell the reader that this is not a complete quotation.)

- _Indirect Quote_: John Smith said that he disagrees with Mark Benson on the results.

- Periods and commas always go inside quotation marks: John Smith said, "I don't think so," and Jane Doe said, "I agree."

- Colons and semicolons always go outside quotation marks: John Smith said he is firmly "committed"; his partner is undecided.

- Single quotation marks are used only within double quotation marks: John Smith said, "James told me, 'I am sure,' before he left."

- When quotations are longer than four lines or 40 words, remove the quotation marks, introduce the quotation, and set the direct quotation off with two indents, as in the following example (for readability, we have indented this example more than 10 spaces or 2 tabs, so that you can see the indent easier in this bulleted section). In _Handbook of Technical Writing_, Alread, Brusaw, and Oliu (2000) explained how to set off quotations:

> Material that is four lines or longer (MLA) or at least 40 words (APA) is usually inset; that is, it is set off from the

body of the text by being indented from the left margin ten spaces (MLA) or five to seven spaces (APA). The quoted passage is spaced the same as the surrounding text and is not enclosed in quotation marks. . . . If you are not following a specific style manual, you may block indent 10 spaces from both the right and left margins for reports and other documents.

3.12   Semicolons

Everyone should have a favorite punctuation mark, in my view. Mine is the semicolon. But semicolons are only used in two ways.

- The first and the most common is between two independent clauses not joined by a conjunction (examples of conjunctions include *and, or, for, so, but, yet*): I am right; you are wrong.

  Often, these sentences contain a transition word or phrase such as *however, furthermore, for example, consequently*, or *moreover*. The semicolon precedes the transitional word or phrase as long as there is a complete sentence both before and after it: I believe I am right; however, I am open to suggestions. I do not, however, agree. (Note that there is a comma after the transitional word when a semicolon precedes it.)

- The second use of the semicolon is to clarify a list that contains commas. The semicolon separates elements that go together. For example: I have lived in Anchorage, Alaska; Eugene, Oregon; New York, New York; and Seattle, Washington.

4.0 COMPANY STYLE

This section lists our "house style" for document text issues. Many of these items are not necessarily "rules" of grammar or punctuation. Instead, the word "style" refers to a company's preferences for how such items as acronyms, commas in a series, capitalization, justification, and italics are used.

There are almost as many styles as there are companies and publications. Newspapers, for example, usually use the Associated Press (AP) style. The styles I have chosen for this style guide is based on standards in the technical writing industry, the *Chicago Manual of Style,* and the Government Printing Office style, as well as the preferences of our clients. These are subject to change. However, it is important to be consistent within documents themselves, and within our company. Therefore, try to follow these style guidelines when writing your document. The technical editor will also look to make sure that all documents meet our style requirements; therefore, do not worry if you are not sure of something or do not have time to check everything. This is the editor's job, and this section is mainly written for editors and document processors to use. This is probably the most important section of this style guide, as it sets down the guidelines for our own company's style.

4.1 Abbreviations and Acronyms

- There is no need to use an abbreviation if a term is only used once. Just spell out the term. (Example: The U.S. Environmental Protection Agency is . . .)

- If using an abbreviation more than once, place it in parentheses after the complete term first appears. From then on, use the abbreviation only. (Example: The U.S. Environmental Protection Agency (USEPA) is . . . According to the USEPA . . .)

- Generally, do not use "the" before abbreviations (example: TPH was detected). Exceptions are certain government agencies (the USEPA, the ADEC).

- Abbreviations and acronyms are generally treated as singular nouns (the USEPA is the agency overseeing the program). Make acronyms plural by adding s (no apostrophe), as in VOCs. Only use the apostrophe for possession (the FDA's position).

- TPH and BTEX are collective nouns that take singular verbs; do not add the "s" to them: Total petroleum hydrocarbons were detected; TPH was detected.

- Do not define U.S., Latin abbreviations (etc.), or compass directions (NE). Some companies prefer not to define F (for Fahrenheit) or C (for Celsius) as well. Abbreviations do not contain periods, except U.S., in., Mr., Ms., no. (number), p. (page), pp. (pages), Latin abbreviations (i.e., et al., etc., e.g.), and degrees (Ph.D., M.A., B.S.).

- Some companies and agencies capitalize all words in their acronyms list, but I do not. I follow the correct capitalization for that term. For example, I capitalize Quality Assurance Plan (QAP) when it is referring to a specific company plan but not when it is referring to such plans in general (QAP is all caps in either case, of course).

- The original words that the acronym represents are not necessarily capitalized; see the abbreviations and acronyms list in Section 13.0 of this document to be sure. (Example: method reporting limit [MRL]).

- Articles agree with the pronunciation of the acronym: an MSDS (em ess dee ess), a RCRA assessment (rik-rah).

- Latin (i.e., e.g., etc.). You do not need to define Latin abbreviations. But do make sure you are using them correctly. i.e. means that is, e.g. means for example, and etc. means and so forth or and so on. Check Merriam-Webster's Tenth New Collegiate Dictionary if you are not sure of the meaning of a Latin abbreviation (see the abbreviations section near the back of the dictionary).

- Always use a comma after i.e. and e.g. Also, they should be used in parenthetical text only: The tanks hold two liquids (i.e., gasoline and methanol).

- If etc. ends a sentence, do not add a second period. Usually you can avoid using etc. by revising the text to include a phrase such as "and others" or "and so on." Another way is to revise the phrase that precedes a list by adding the word includes or including. Instead of writing *The mammals I saw were moose, elk, rabbits, etc.* write *The mammals I saw included moose, elk, and rabbits.*

- Treat résumés, executive summaries, transmittal letters, and figures and tables as separate documents. Redefine acronyms and abbreviations in them. Provide a key to all acronyms and abbreviations used in the tables and figures; the key goes at the bottom of the table or figure.

Section 13.0 contains lists of commonly used acronyms and abbreviations in this field. However, you may find that some have changed or that your company has others to add to this list. If searching on the Internet for the correct spelling, capitalization, and usage of an acronym or abbreviation, I prefer to find government agency Web sites for sources. You will find many errors online, of course, and it may take some searching to find a reliable source. By including the acronyms and abbreviations sections in this document, I hope to have saved you time.

4.2   Companies and Agencies

- Use the name as the company or agency does on its official documents. It may contain and, &, Inc., Co., or Company.

- You can shorten Company to Co. and Incorporated to Inc.

- Usually there is a comma before "Inc.," but if the company is not using a comma in its official documents, leave it out.

- A company is singular, so it takes a singular verb. Also, if you use a pronoun to reference the company, use "it" instead of "they."

  Example: Champion Word Services is skilled in providing detailed editing to corporate documents. It is also . . .

  Since the word "it" is a bit awkward sounding, this is a good place to use an acronym [CWS] as long as it is defined previously; to use "The company"; to use the company's full name again; or to combine the two sentences and eliminate the need for the subject to be repeated (e.g., Champion Word Services is skilled in providing detailed editing of corporate documents and in providing quality workshops to corporate personnel).

4.3   Company, Software, and Equipment Names

As a technical editor, you will find it useful to keep lists of items you use frequently in documents, including the following:

- acronyms and abbreviations;

- previous projects (with exact titles);

- company names (including subcontractors that you might use in proposals, for example);

- software titles; and

- equipment (again, you might list these in proposals).

Although I have included an acronyms list at the end of this document, company names are so numerous and varied that it will be necessary to create your own.

I often see inconsistency in company and product names in documents, which is why I added this section. Specific inconsistencies are seen in capitalization, spelling, and spacing of equipment and software names. The purpose of this list is to provide an accurate, exact list of all of company, software, and equipment names; keep the list updated; and avoid confusion and inconsistencies in your documents.

Below, I have provided some examples from company, software, and equipment based on hydrographic surveying, for an example of what you might create for your own company.

4.3.1   Company Names Examples

The following company spellings, for example, including capitalization, spelling, hyphenation, were checked on company Web sites. Whenever possible, I included in my list the company Web site address for checking additional products, updating names, and other questions.

Triton Elics International (can use Triton or TEI for multiple uses; just define first use)

Products:

BathyPro™
Bathy+Plus™
DelphMap™
DelphNav™

Delph Seismic®+Plus

HydroSuite™

Isis® Sonar

SeaClass™

SGIS™

Thales GeoSolutions Group Ltd.

Thales Geosolutions (Pacific) Inc.

Trimble®

4.3.2 Equipment Names

These equipment names have been taken directly from company Web sites, so the spacing, spelling, capitalization, and the use of the TM or R symbols should be correct. Whenever possible, I have inserted the company (manufacturer's) name in parentheses after the equipment or software name. The rule on the ™ or ® symbol is to either use the symbol throughout the document or to use it at least the first time the product is mentioned in a document (the company would no doubt prefer the first technique, but for proposals, I usually use the second; for published reports, I use the first [i.e., list TM or R symbol with every mention]).

AutoCAD

AutoCAD/MAP

Bathy+Plus™ (Triton Elics International)

BathyPro™ (Triton Elics International)

CARIS®

CARIS® HIPS

CARIS® SIPS

Delph Seismic®+Plus (Triton Elics International)

DelphMap™ (Triton Elics International)

DelphNav™ (Triton Elics International)

Echotrac (use Odom Echotrac)

ESRI

HydroBat (Reson software)

HydroSuite™ (Triton Elics International)

HYPACK®

HYPACK® MAX

Isis® (side-scan sonar acquisition system made by Triton Elics International)

Isis® Sonar (Triton Elics International)

MapInfo

MicroStation (made by Bentley Systems Inc.)

Morad Electronics Corp. (manufacturer of antennas)

Odom

Odom Echotrac (a dual-frequency survey echo sounder)

ORE Offshore

ORE Offshore Trackpoint (Be specific: Trackpoint 4440A or Trackpoint II; give full name if possible)

Polaris Imaging

Polaris Imaging EOSCAN® (a sonar data acquisition and display system)

Reson (full name of U.S. company: Reson Inc.)

SeaBat (Reson software)

SeaClass™ (Triton Elics International)

Seapath 200 (made by Seatex Inc.)

SGISTM (Triton Elics International)

Tripod Data Systems (a Trimble® company)

Triton Elics International (can use Triton or TEI for multiple uses; just define first use)

Triton Isis®

WaterLOG®

WinFrog (Thales Geosolutions)

4.4   Dates

- Do not add letters to a date: June 27, not June 27th.

- Do not shorten: 1970s, not '70s

- Use a comma with month, day, and year: August 18, 1999, was the date of the test.

- Do not abbreviate months in text (okay in figures and tables): December, not Dec.

- Only use an apostrophe with a date if it is possessive. Examples: The 1990s were very good years. In my experience, 1974's best song was "Me and Mrs. Jones."

4.5   Headings and Titles

- Capitalize the first word, the major parts of speech (nouns, adjectives, adverbs, and verbs), other parts of speech with four or more letters (including prepositions with four or more letters), and the last word in all levels of headings: Memory in Hearing-Impaired Children, On-Site Wells, Playing With Fire.

- Do not use 0.0, 0.1, 0.2, etc. as a chapter heading. The first chapter should begin with "1," as in 1.0, 1.1, 1.2, etc. The Transmittal Letter, the Abbreviations and Acronym List, and the Executive Summary do not have heading numbers.

- The following are the fonts normally used in standard company reports. You do not need to format the fonts; they are provided here for your information. The technical editor or document processer will take care of this. You also should never number your headings; this is automatically done by document processing using the styles feature in Microsoft Word.

  - Caps, Centered, bold, Arial 14, *number at left is 4.0*

  - All caps, left justified, bold, Arial 12, *number at left is 4.1*

  - Upper and lowercase, left, bold, Arial 11, *number at left is 4.1.1*

  - Upper and lowercase, number is indented .5 (1 tab), no bold, italic, Arial 10, *number at left is 4.1.1.1*

  - Fifth-level heading. Italics, Arial 10, underlined, *do not use number at left*

4.5.1   Heading Introductions

Always write at least a one-sentence introduction under a heading title before going on to another heading title. For example: This section describes the 2002 remediation activities at the Bethel Landfill.

4.6   Italics

- Generally, avoid italics in formal writing, except for the following examples.

  - Italicize the names of vessels: the *Exxon Valdez*.

— Italicize the taxonomic names of genera, species, and varieties: The mountain is covered by second-growth forests of Douglas fir (*Pseudotsuga menziesii*).

— Italicize foreign words and phrases only if they have not yet entered common usage (do not italicize in situ; this is commonly used).

— In the text and in the reference list, italicize titles of major documents; do not use quotation marks around such titles: *Final Report: Bethel Landfill Cleanup*. When you refer to chapters or articles within larger works (such as an article within a journal), use quotation marks around the shorter work's title: In "The Story of the Essay," from Jane Doe's *English Secrets*, we learn that every successful essay has a thesis. Do not put quotation marks around section titles of reports, however. Example: Section 1.0 of this document contains an overview of the work performed.

- Do not italicize punctuation that precedes or follows italicized words or sections.

- Do not italicize punctuation before or after an italicized word, just those that are part of the italicized material.

4.7   Justification

You have two choices with company style: left justification or full justification. Some believe that full justification looks more professional. Tests reveal that left justification (i.e., ragged right) is more readable, especially with lengthy and technical material. Therefore, it is acceptable to use ragged right in your company documents.

4.8   Lists (Bulleted and Numbered Lists)

Bullet styles vary from company to company and from style book to style book. These are guidelines for our company documents but are always subject to change. For now, these are our preferences.

- Generally, bullets are preferred to numbers for lists. Numbers can be used in sequential steps.

- Perhaps most important is the introductory sentence or phrase to the list. Again, there are lots of styles and discussions on this, but for consistency, the following outlines our company's preferred style. It is up to you, or to the editor, whether to use a colon after the last word preceding the bullet list even though the sentence might be a fragment (e.g., The three tests run were:). If you can make a complete sentence to precede the colon, this is preferred. One way to do this is to add the words "the following" to the clause you have and then use a colon. Example: The methods used will include the following:

- Note that if you use the word "include" or "including" in your introductory sentence, you have an incomplete list following. Drop the "include" if you have a complete list. The animals seen included wolves, moose, and ptarmigan. (Other animals were also seen.) The animals seen were wolves, moose, and ptarmigan. (No other animals were seen.)

- It is important that each bullet item be parallel to the others. Therefore, if one is a complete sentence with a period, the others should all be complete sentences with periods.

- If each bullet item is not a complete sentence, do not use periods. Also, make sure they each follow the introductory sentence (i.e., that they make sense when joined with the introductory sentence).

- If you use commas at the end of the bullet items, add the word "and" after the last comma (i.e., the second to last bullet item), and insert a period at the end of the last bullet item.

- If there are commas within bulleted items, but the entire bullet list is part of a complete sentence, use semicolons instead of commas at the end of each bullet item (and a period at the end).

- Capitalize the first word of each item in a list if each item is a complete sentence or is lengthy. Include the period as well in these cases. Do not capitalize the first word and use commas (or semicolons as described above) if the bullet items consist of one or a few words and merely complete the sentence introducing them. For example:

  Laboratory quality control (QC) samples will include:
  - method blanks,

- laboratory control sample duplicates, and
- matrix spike duplicate samples.

4.9   Measurements

- Use figures (i.e., don't spell out) for numbers that refer to measurements: 8 cm wide, 9 percent, 8 years old, 5-mg dose, 4 miles, 6 minutes, 3 inches, 7 acres.

- Spell out simple units in the text, such as inch, acre, liter, minute, and year. But if they are part of a complex unit, use the abbreviation (define first use just as you would with any abbreviation): ft/min, mg/L.

- Abbreviated measurements are written the same whether singular or plural. For example, lb can refer to both pound and pounds.

- Most measurement abbreviations do not take a period. Some do, however (in. for inch). See the list of measurement abbreviations in Section 13.0 to be sure.

4.10   Numbers

- Generally, spell out numbers less than 10 (one, three), and use numerals for 10 and higher (14, 256).

- Always use numerals to express measurement (2 feet, 4 mg/L, 7 gmp, 5 pore volumes), time (10 p.m.), parts of a document (Chapter 4, Phase 4, Section 2, Item 3, Table 6-1, Figure 2-3), money ($3 million), very large numbers followed by million or billion (7 million), percentages and decimal fractions (3 percent, 3.14, 1.2), and ratios (1 to 10).

- When two or more numbers are listed in a group in the same sentence, and one or more is 10 or more, use numerals for all:

  — The laboratory evaluated 7 of the 12 samples.

  — The contractor drilled 12 borings to a depth of 70 feet and completed 4 of the 12 borings as vapor extraction wells.

  — The contractor drilled six borings to a depth of 70 feet and completed four of the six borings as vapor extraction wells.

- Spell out all numbers that start a sentence: Twelve test holes were analyzed. You can also rewrite the sentence to move the number: *XYZ Company* analyzed 12 test holes.

- When numbers appear together in the same phrase, it is often a good practice to express one as a word and one as a number (*XYZ Company* purchased fourteen 8-inch pipes) but not in a list (*XYZ Company* purchased 6-, 8-, and 12-inch pipes).

- Use a comma in numbers larger than 999: 12,000, 9,000, 800.

- Use Arabic (1, 2, 3), not Roman (I, II, III), numerals for figures, illustrations, and tables.

- Change Roman numerals to Arabic in references, even when Roman numerals are used in the work itself: (Example: USEPA Region 10, Phase 3).

4.11   Parallelism

This is an important—albeit confusing—topic for technical writers, especially since we use so many lists. Basically, the elements in a list must all have the same grammatical structure. They must each flow individually from the introductory sentence. Make sure all the elements in a bulleted list, for example, are parallel to each other. If you begin one item with a verb, for example, all items must begin with a verb. The beginning of a list is the most important part; if necessary, it is acceptable to add additional elements to one or more items (see final example, below).

Incorrect: I like to do the following: flying an airplane, ride a bicycle, and shooting a gun.

Correct: I like to do the following: flying an airplane, riding a bicycle, and shooting a gun.

Incorrect: My dog is old, ugly, and he has a disease.

Correct: My dog is old, ugly, and diseased.

Incorrect: Approximately half the landfill was open to the public, and 25 percent was under development.

Correct: Approximately 50 percent of the landfill was open to the public, and 25 percent was under development.

Incorrect:
- Drill borings
- Installing wells
- Collection of samples

Correct:
- Drill borings
- Install wells
- Collect samples

Incorrect:

The objectives of this investigation were as follows:

- To determine the extent of petroleum-hydrocarbon impacted soils in the areas of confirmed impact.

- Determining the potential presence of petroleum-hydrocarbon impact to soil and water along the eastern edge of the pad.

- Collect subsurface hydrogeologic information.

- Collect such data as may be necessary, including identifying physical characteristics of the site, to support development of corrective actions and RBCLs, if warranted.

Correct:

The objectives of this investigation were as follows:

- To determine the extent of petroleum-hydrocarbon impacted soils in the areas of confirmed impact.

- To determine the potential presence of petroleum-hydrocarbon impact to soil and water along the eastern edge of the pad.

- To collect subsurface hydrogeologic information.

- To collect such data as may be necessary, including identifying physical characteristics of the site, to support development of corrective actions and RBCLs, if warranted.

4.12 References in the Text

- All that is necessary in the text is the author's last name and the year of publication (Smith, 1989). The complete information is found in the reference section. However, if you choose to give the author's full name first use or to list the title, that is acceptable.

- Use a semicolon to separate two or more references in the text (XYZ Company, 1993; USEPA, 1999).

- If the same author has more than one publication from the same year listed in the references section, use "a," "b," etc. (XYZ Company, 1999a).

- Note that commas follow the last name in our company's style (Jones, 2000).

4.13 Spacing

- Our company's style is to put one space after a period.

- There should only be one space after a comma, semicolon, or colon.

- The spacing of ellipsis points is (space) dot (space) dot (space) dot (space). Example: Mr. Rogers said that "easy children are . . . wonderful."

- The spacing of ellipsis points with an end period is (no space) dot (space) dot (space) dot (space). Example: According to NOAA, "The data are incomplete. . . ."

4.14 Spelling

- Use *Merriam-Webster's New Collegiate Dictionary* (m-w.com) as a standard spelling reference. If there is a choice of two spellings, use the first one (for example, canceled rather than cancelled).

- A list of commonly misspelled words is included in the Section 10.0 of this style guide.

- Watch for the following plurals, and remember that plural nouns take plural verbs. Singular: datum, matrix, phenomenon, schema. Plural: data, matrices, phenomena, schemas. The data are, the datum is . . .

4.14.1 Change British Spelling to American English

If you are asked to edit a British document for an American company, or vice versa, this list (Table 4-1) of the main differences between British and American spelling should make your task easier.

Table 4-1   British and American Spelling Differences

British	American
-our (vapour, colour)	-or (vapor, color)
-re (centre, metre)	-er (center, meter)
-ogue (dialogue)	-og (dialog)
-ence (defence)	-ense (defense)
-ise (minimise)	-ize (minimize)
-ising (utilising)	-izing (utilizing)
-isation (utilization)	-ization (utilization)
-isance (cognisance)	-izance (cognizance)
manoeuvred	maneuvered
learnt	learned
traveller	traveler
modelled	modeled
aluminium	aluminum
sulphide	sulfide
whilst	while
programme	program
judgement	judgment
towards	toward

American English spelling sometimes does not double the consonant at the end of a word, while British English spelling does, especially when the consonant is an "L"; for example, *travel, traveller, travelling* (U.K.) and *travel, traveler, traveling* (U.S.).

Also, note that U.S. English differs for the following (these are U.S.): single quotes inside double quotes, brackets inside parentheses.

4.15 Temperatures

- Use the numeral, the degree symbol, and either "F" or "C" for temperatures. Example: The temperature was 14 °F inside the building.

- Be consistent with using either F or C. U.S. companies will often give the temperature in Fahrenheit first, then in Celsius in parentheses, as in the following example:

  − The water temperature shall not be less than 40 °F (4.4 °C).

- The correct definitions and spellings are Fahrenheit (F) and Celsius (C). Some companies use "Centigrade" instead of "Celsius," but our company's style is to use Celsius.

4.16 Tense

In general, technical writers use present tense unless referring to past events. In those cases, use past tense. Proposals will probably also use future tense (*XYZ Company will evaluate the data*). Refer to other sources in past tense (*Smith said that . . .*). Discuss past results of tests in past tense (*One water sample was analyzed for VOCs*). Discuss final results and conclusions in present tense (*the results indicate*). Following are examples of correct tense usage:

- John Smith said, "I don't think so."

- The landfill was evaluated by Jane Doe, who said at the time, "There are clear violations here."

- Janet Smith, in *The Making of a Great Disposal Area*, wrote, "Efficiency is the most important thing."

- If the participant is finished answering the questions, the data are complete.

- Since that time, investigators from several studies have used this method.

- The CERCLA investigation includes the following. . . .

- Successfully completing site investigation or RI/FS projects has been the subcontractor's main focus since 1990.

- The group was formed to provide a core of specialists to the FAA. . . .

- The company's field staff members are trained to . . .

- Examples of site investigations XYZ Company has performed in Alaska include. . . .

- This report includes seven sections and two appendices.

- Section 1.0 contains the report introduction. . . .

- XYZ Company is recognized as a leading groundwater consulting firm.

4.17 Time

- Use a.m. and p.m. (note lowercase and periods) when included with the time: 10 a.m.

- Do not define a.m. and p.m.

- Use numerals when referring to a specific time, even if the number is less than 10. Example: The company ran the test at 3 p.m. and again at 9 p.m.

- Do not put two periods next to each other, even if a.m. or p.m. end the sentence. Example: The company ran a final test at 1 a.m.

- Do not put o'clock or :00 after the time if it is on the hour (Example: Sample collection occurred between 11 a.m. and 1 p.m.). But do use a colon and a numeral when giving specific times that are not on the hour (Examples: 2:15 p.m., 4:32 a.m.).

- If you are referring to a nonspecific time, do not use a.m. or p.m. Example: The company representatives arrived in the afternoon. But generally, in technical writing, we try to be exact, so use the correct time if you can.

4.18 Titles and Names of People

- Capitalize titles only when they directly precede a person's name or are part of an address: The source of the information was Project Manager Jane Szmanski. The project manager is Jane Szmanski. Jane Szmanski, project manager, is . . .

- Do not use a hyphen in vice president.

- In the text, give the person's full name the first mention. From then on, use Mr. or Ms. before the last name. If you are not sure of the person's gender, continue using the full name. Examples: John Smith, Mr. Smith; Sally Jones, Ms. Jones; Pat Johnson, Pat Johnson.

4.19   Unbiased Language

By now we all know we should write language that is inoffensive, but sometimes it is difficult to know what to replace words with. Sometimes the correction may seem wordy or awkward. Often the simplest way to avoid using *he/she* or *he and she* is to make the subject plural. For example, replace "An English teacher has little time to read anything except his or her students' papers" with "English teachers have little time to read anything except student papers." Modern English handbooks contain many suggestions for revising to eliminate biased language. Table 4-1 contains examples from the *Publication Manual of the American Psychological Association.*

Table 4-2   Replacing Biased Language with Unbiased Language

Replace:	With:
The client is the best judge of his counseling.	Clients are the best judges of the counseling they receive. The client is the best judge of the value of counseling.
man, mankind	people, humanity, human beings, humankind, humans
man a project	staff a project, hire personnel, employ staff
manpower	workforce, personnel, workers, human resources
woman doctor, lady lawyer, male nurse, woman driver	physician, lawyer, nurse, driver
chairman	chair, chairperson
foreman	supervisor or superintendent
Eskimos	Inuit, Aleuts (be specific)
disabled person, mentally ill person	person with a disability, person with mental illness
stroke victim, suffering from multiple sclerosis, confined to a wheelchair	individual who had a stroke, people who have multiple sclerosis, uses a wheelchair

Source: *Publication Manual of the American Psychological Association*

5.0   WRITING TIPS

The purpose of this section is to help you make your writing sharp and clear and to point out common errors to avoid, such as using clichés.

5.1   Overview

No matter what type of writing you are doing, technical or not, consider two things as most important: (1) audience, and (2) ethos (or your writer's tone; how you come across). Try to consider your audience when you write, and do not expect your readers to be experts in your subject matter or to know the definitions of the terms, acronyms, and abbreviations you are using. At the same time, consider your "ethos" by not writing "down" to your audience. You want to approach your subject matter with both respect for the readers and clarity.

Often, as a technical editor, my job is to tell the author, "This doesn't make sense to me here. Can you clarify?" I represent the "nonexpert" audience, and I try to read from this perspective, so I can tell the writer exactly where the writing might "lose" the readers.

You, as the writer, and an expert on the subject, might know what you mean, but did you really explain it to the reader in a clear, concise manner? Other questions to consider include:

- Are all tables and figures explained fully in the text before they appear?

- Do the tables make sense on their own?

- Can the reader follow your organization?

Outlines can be handy tools to use before actually writing, as discussed in Section 4.5. Personally, I prefer to make an outline before I am going to write technical material. Your outline can be just a few notes, a list of major (and perhaps minor) headings, or a full-on list of every paragraph in the document. Whatever helps you organize the material best is the method to use.

It may be necessary to go back after writing and reorganize sections. Some writers work better getting the material down quickly, and then going back and reshaping it.

If you are "stuck," or feel that your document is not flowing well, do not hesitate to ask the technical editor for help.

5.2   Getting Started

Here are some tips that may help you get started in writing your document. An English handbook also provides many ideas for beginning the writing process, outlining your ideas, and organizing your material. Therefore, if you have "writer's block," it might also be useful to look through those sections in a handbook. Here are steps to take before you begin writing:

1. Gather information and data (think about what you want to say).

2. Identify and refine your document's purpose (consider why you are going to say it).

3. Identify your audience (determine who you are going to say it to).

4. Organize your information and ideas (decide how you are going to say it).

For Step 4, it is useful to make an outline. Your outline can be changed, of course, but it will often lead you to knowing your headings and subheadings and where to put specific material in your document. A writer might find it easier to write the outline as a Table of Contents page.

The next step is actually writing the draft. You can write sections out of order, if needed. Do not worry about grammar, punctuation, and style at this point. Just get something down.

After you have your draft written, go ahead and do your revisions. If you have time to set it aside a day, go ahead and do so. As you revise, aim to clarify, strengthen, and condense your message. Also, check the overall organization. This is also the time to go back and write the introductory material, such as the Transmittal Letter and Executive Summary, if needed in this report.

As you revise, here are some questions that might assist you:

- Does the reader know what the report, section, or paragraph is about? If not, make sure you have the topic sentences or main ideas listed first. Example: "This section evaluates the data collected from the three well sites."

- What does the audience most likely want to know? Check any materials you have (bid packet, report guidelines, previous reports, original proposal) to make sure you have provided the necessary information.

- How well organized is the document?

- Are there any gaps in logic or information?

- Is there enough supporting material (i.e., figures, tables, graphs)?

- Did you use transitional words and phrases (therefore, furthermore, for example, however, in fact, also, first, second, finally, consequently, in addition, on the other hand, next, in conclusion, as a result, in the same way, in other words, in contrast, most important, further, to summarize)?

- How well did you say it? Do you have awkward sentences? Have you checked for the following problem areas (this is also done by the technical editor): sentence structure, sentence variety, subject-verb agreement, passive voice, wordiness, misuse of pronouns, misplaced modifiers, faulty parallelism, poor organization, and poor formatting? Use your handbook or this style guide for suggestions on improving these areas.

- Did you leave anything out that is essential to fulfilling the requirements of the document?

- Did you include information that is not relevant?

- Did you use specific, concrete language? Can a nonexpert read your document?

- Did you avoid jargon, clichés, and wordiness?

- Did you use enough headings and bullet lists to add to readability?

5.3   Active and Passive Voice

"Don't use passive voice," is probably one of those red-ink English teacher comments you sometimes saw but that was never explained. Active voice is preferred because it is easier to read and to understand, so it is especially important in technical material. Basically, in the active voice, the subject comes first. Another way to look at it is that the subject does the acting.

ACTIVE: The contractor evaluated the data.

In passive voice, the subject is acted upon. The reason this is a problem is that it is wordy and harder to follow.

PASSIVE: The data were evaluated by the contractor.

5.4   Be Specific

Technical writers should be as clear and specific as possible, avoiding vague language. Therefore, if you are seeing words like "many, some, a few" in a document, it probably needs revising. Instead of writing "a very high concentration," for example, give the exact measurement. Give the depth of a test pit rather than just calling it "shallow" or "deep." Instead of merely saying something is "contaminated," provide the reader with the amount by which the standard is exceeded and specifically name the compounds involved. Instead of saying something is satisfactory, state exactly which standards or regulations it meets.

5.5   Clichés

Avoid clichés like the plague; they are overused expressions that have lost their meaning. Even if you are blind as a bat, you can see a cliché for what it is: nothing.

5.6   Jargon

One of the main goals of technical writers is to make text clear and simple. One of the ways this is done is by replacing jargon with simple, clear language. Jargon is technical vocabulary, and it is often not necessary. One of the best things to happen to technical writing in the last 20 years is the elimination of jargon and the increase in readability of documents. Writing jargon or extra words (such as this example from APA: "monetarily felt scarcity" instead of "poverty") prevents readers from understanding the text. Here is an example from another company's style guide:

> Winston Churchill, facing Hitler's armed forces in 1940, said to Americans, "Give us the tools, and we will do the job." He did not say, "Supply us with the necessary

inputs of relevant equipment, and we will implement the program and accomplish its objectives."

Table 5-1 contains examples of jargon and ways to correct them.

Table 5-1   Simplifying Jargon

Replace	With
adjacent to	next to, beside, near, adjoining
atop	on
currently	now
per your request	as requested
observed	saw
presently	now
prior to	before
with regard to, relating to	about, for, of
reside	live
residential structure	residence
stated	said
subsequent to	after
upon	on
usage	use
utilize	use
with respect to	about

Source: *Chicago Manual of Style*

5.7   Sentence Errors

Comma splices, fragments, and run-on sentences are the three most common sentence errors. Any English handbook contains detailed definitions of each of these, but here are examples for your reference.

Comma Splice: A comma splice has a complete sentence before the comma, it also has a complete sentence after the comma.

How to correct: Use a period or a semicolon instead of a comma, or add a coordinating conjunction after the comma (and, but, or, for, so, yet).

Fragment: An incomplete thought. Fragments are unfinished because. All sentences need, at a minimum. A subject and a verb.

How to correct: If it sounds incomplete, it is probably a fragment. Revise the sentence.

Run-ons: Run-on sentences are two sentences crashed together they have no punctuation in between them.

How to correct: The easiest way to correct run-on sentences is to put a period or semicolon in between the two sentences.

5.8   Vague Terms

Try to avoid using "it" and vague pronoun references. State exactly who or what you mean.

CONFUSING: Columbia Analytical Services gave the results to XYZ Company. It then gave the results to the client's representatives. They . . .

CLARIFIED: Columbia Analytical Services gave the results to XYZ Company. XYZ Company gave a copy of the results to the client, Company A. Company A then . . .

Also, note that a company is singular, so you would not use "they" when referring to a company. This is where you will sometimes use "it," but make sure your text is clear on who or what "it" refers to.

5.9   Wordiness

Technical writing should be "tight" and clear. If you can use one word instead of three or four, do so. The main problem with wordiness is that it makes the text hard to read. Table 5-2 shows some shorter alternatives to wordy phrases such as using "for" instead of "for the purposes of."

Another way to eliminate wordiness is to avoid redundant phrases. In the following examples from APA, the italicized words are redundant and should be eliminated: *one and* the same, in *close* proximity, *completely* unanimous, *period of* time, summarize *briefly*, the reason is *because*, has been *previously* found, small *in size*, *a total of* 68 participants, *both* alike, four *different* groups.

Table 5-2   Eliminating Wordiness

Wordy Phrase	Better
a 7-year period	7 years
a large number of	many

Wordy Phrase	Better
ahead of schedule	early
as to whether	whether
at this point in time	now
based on the fact that	because
blue in color	blue
close proximity	proximity
conduct interviews with	interview
consensus of opinion	consensus
constructed in two levels	two-story
contained within	in
designated, termed, named as	designated, termed, named
developed for residential use	residential
divided into four quarters	divided into quarters
during the time that	while, when
end product	product
few in number	few
fine-grained in texture	fine-grained
first priority	priority
for the purpose of assessing	to assess
for the purpose of	for, to
future potential	potential
immediately adjacent to	next to, beside, adjoining
in a shingle-type method	like shingles
in advance of	before
in excess of	over, exceeding
in order to accomplish	to accomplish
in proximity to	near
in regard to, in relation to	regarding, about, of
in the event that	if
in the near future	soon
in the vicinity of	near, about
infiltrate through	infiltrate
integral part	part
is in a muddy condition	is muddy
is to be established	will be established

Wordy Phrase	Better
it is *Company*'s understanding	*Company* understands
may, might possibly	may, might
of a similar nature, similar in nature	similar
on a monthly (weekly) basis	monthly (weekly)
on an as-needed basis	as needed
performed a site reconnaissance	reconnoitered (the site)
prior to the collection of samples	before samples are collected
results so far achieved	results so far
the present study	this study
there were several students who completed	12 students completed
to the point that	enough, sufficiently
topographic features	topography
were used for the storage of	stored
work, tasks performed	work, tasks

Source: *Chicago Manual of Style*

5.10 Words to Avoid for Liability Reasons

Try to avoid overstating or overpromising. Be careful with word selection. Make sure if you use the following words and ones similar to them that you are not promising or saying too much: all, none, always, never, any, eliminate, stop, equal, guarantee, warrant, certify, ensure, insure, best, highest, maximum, minimum.

There are other words available in this rich English language that should serve your purposes just as well, depending on the context, such as sufficient, typical, facilitate, monitor, equivalent, similar, limit, reduce, recommend, and review.

Here is an example: Instead of *XYZ Company guarantees to provide the client with the best choice*, write *XYZ Company will advise the client on the most appropriate action.*

6.0   STANDARD DOCUMENT FORMATTING

Overall, most companies prefer block format for all technical documents. Block format means that paragraphs are single spaced (or perhaps 1.15 as shown on Figure 6-1, below), with a full paragraph space above (also shown on Figure 6-1; in this case, I inserted 12 points above each paragraph and 0 points below; this would be standard when the font size for "normal" text in the document is also 12 points). Headings should also have 12 points above and 0 points below.

Most companies seem to prefer left justification for reports and other documents as well. This is easier to read. However, full justification can look more professional, so this is your decision.

There should only be one space after a period, colon, or semicolon. This changed since the "typewriter days," when two spaces were called for after a period. Now it is easy to search and replace two spaces with one throughout an entire document.

I have formatted the book form of this document to model what I suggest:

- Times New Roman 11-point font for normal text.

- Arial bold font for headings

- One space after periods, commas, and semicolons.

- Block format (11 points above each single-spaced paragraph).

- Figure and table captions before the figure and table, and always referenced in the text before they appear. (Note that some disagree with me on this and still put the figure captions below, or after, the figure. As an editor, I accept and use the company's style I am working with. But I prefer to have the caption before the figure so that I can add notes below the figure and so that a short title can be used that will be included in the automated Table of Contents.)

Figure 6-1   Paragraph Spacing for Technical Documents

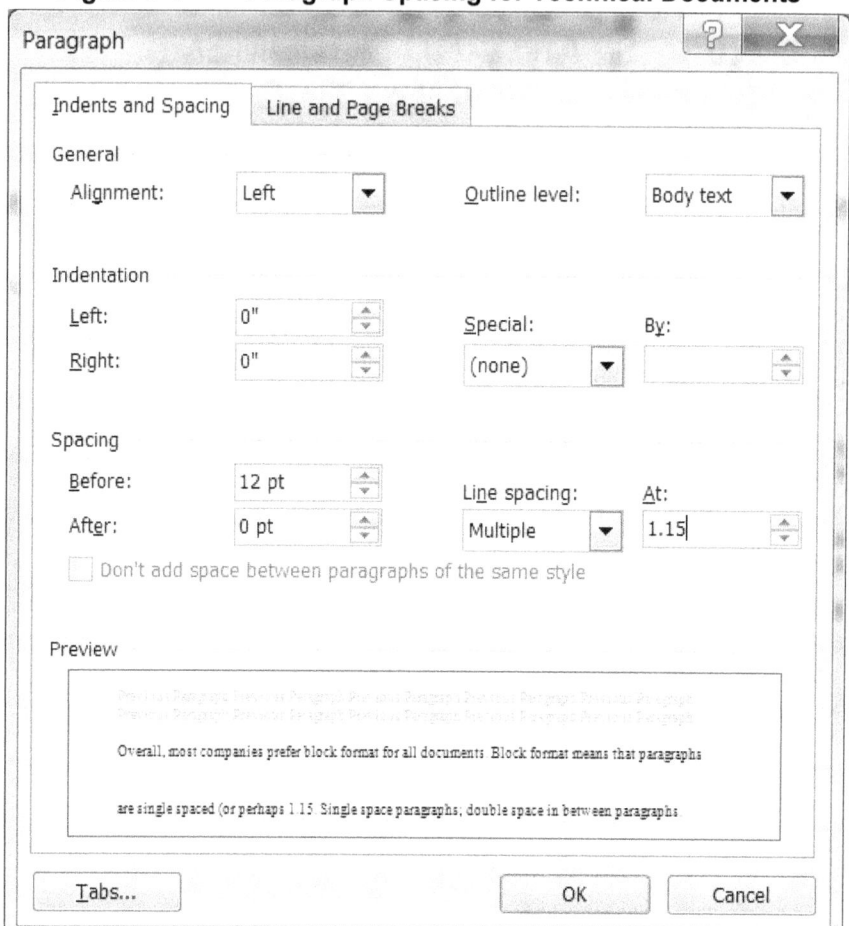

6.1   Memorandum

The standard format for memoranda is as follows:

Margins: 1 inch from top, bottom, and both sides.

Justification: Memos are fully justified.

Font: Text font is Times New Roman 11 points.

Use your company's stationery.

Introductory material: The template has the necessary information in the following order:

Date:

To:

From:

Subject:

Signature: Memos are not signed.

Spacing: single-spaced paragraphs with a double space between each paragraph.

End: At the end of a memo, always include the following:

Attachments

Enclosures (if any)

cc: file (and any other names or places copies are going)

Length: A memo should only be one or two pages; if more than one page, consider using a letter format instead.

6.2   Transmittal Letter

A transmittal letter is sometimes included in the front matter of a lengthy (40 or more pages) report. Here are some features of the transmittal letter:

- A letter is usually one page. Short one-page letters usually have three paragraphs: introduction, body, and closing.

- The language is not technical.

- The letter documents when the report was sent, how it was sent, to whom it was addressed, how many copies were sent, and who was responsible for preparing the report.

- A letter does not use acronyms and abbreviations.

- The letter is addressed to a specific person (Dear Mr. Jones:).

- Distribution is noted on the bottom left (cc.).

- The letter also clarifies if it is a draft report, and, if so, when comments are due back and how.

- The letter indicates, if it is a draft, what is missing from the report (if anything) and when the missing information will be available.

- The letter closes by thanking the client and using the word "Sincerely,".

6.3   Standard Report

6.3.1   Document Organization

The standard document contains the following elements in this order:

- Title page

- Any preface materials (such as a transmittal letter)

- Table of Contents

- List of Appendices

- List of Figures and Tables

- List of Acronyms and Abbreviations

- Section 1.0 Executive Summary

- Section 2.0 Introduction

- Other sections, leading up to the Conclusions and Recommendations Section

- References

- Appendices

6.3.2   Spacing and Text Fonts

- Use single space text.

- Use Times New Roman 11 point font.

- If we use 11-point font, set "normal" style for 11 points before each paragraph for block paragraphing. If we use 12-point font, set normal for 12 points above (or before) each paragraph.

- Use only one space after a period, semicolon, or colon.

- Text should be left justification; shorter company documents may be fully justified.

6.3.3 Section Headings

Each section contains up to five levels of headings, which are formatted as follows:

- Caps, centered, bold, Arial 14, NUMBER AT LEFT IS 4.0

- All caps, left justified, bold, Arial 12, NUMBER AT LEFT IS 4.1

- Upper and lowercase, left, bold, Arial 11, NUMBER AT LEFT IS 4.1.1

- Upper and lowercase, number is indented .5 (1 tab), no bold, italic, Arial 10, NUMBER AT LEFT IS 4.1.1.1

- Fifth-level heading. Italics, Arial 10, underlined, DON'T USE NUMBER AT LEFT

The Table of Contents should be formatted so that only headings 1 through 3 are shown there.

Title Page

The title page should include the following:

- Report title

- Type of report (interim, internal, progress, draft, final)

- Contract, delivery, and job order numbers

- Date

- Client (Prepared for) name and address

- Client logo if available

- Company Name (Prepared by) name and address

- Terra logo

Table of Contents Page

- The header, **TABLE OF CONTENTS**, should be centered and bold.

- Items in the Table of Contents (TOC) should be all caps or initial caps, just as they appear in the text headings.

- No bold or underscores are used in the TOC.

- Second and third-level headings are indented.

- TOCs use up to third-level headings.

- Multivolume reports should each have their own individual TOCs.

List of Tables and Figures

- Use the heading "**LIST OF TABLES AND FIGURES**" all bold and caps at top of the page.

- Begin the List of Tables and Figures on a separate page from the TOC.

- Numbering is handled with hyphens: Figure 1-1.

- Items are in upper/lowercase (title case), no bold.

- If you use the caption command correctly in the text, you should never have to type in the titles and page numbers; just insert the Table of Contents, Tables, and then the Table of Contents, Figures.

List of Appendices

- The List of Appendices (if needed) is placed after the List of Tables and Figures. If it fits, it can be on the same page as the List of Tables and Figures (see example, next page).

- Use the following format for the Appendices TOC:

LIST OF APPENDICES

Appendix A   Title Here

Appendix B   Title Here

- Note that no page numbers are listed for the List of Appendices since they do not actually have page numbers. If they are lengthy documents of themselves that do include page numbers, number each page as A-1, A-2, etc. for Appendix A, and B-1, B-2, etc. for Appendix B.

List of Acronyms and Abbreviations

- Our company places the acronyms list at the front of the document, between the TOC and the Executive Summary. (Some documents are different; for example, Site Technical Practices [CRTs and STPs] include the Abbreviations and Acronyms as Section 4.)

- All acronyms used in the report, including in figures, tables, and appendices, must be included.

- Use the acronyms and abbreviations list in Section 13.0 of this style guide for guidance on capitalization and spelling.

- Be sure the entries are in alphabetical order.

Executive Summary

- Reports more than 40 pages should have an Executive Summary. It is helpful to the reader to have an Executive Summary even if the report is shorter than 40 pages.

- The Executive Summary states the purpose and nature of the investigation; provides a brief account of the approach used; and includes the major results, conclusions, and recommendations.

- The Executive Summary has its own page numbers in the format "ES-#," as in ES-1, ES-2, etc. This emphasizes that the Executive Summary can stand alone.

- Acronyms are defined in the Executive Summary as if it is a separate document that will stand on its own. Do not use them heavily.

- Though unusual in an Executive Summary, if you include Tables or Figures, number them as follows: Figure ES-1.

Report Pages

- Each main section begins on a right-hand page.

- Page numbering is based on the section. For example, page 3-2 means Section 3, page 2.

- Documents are normally printed on both sides of the page if the report is longer than 50 pages.

- Blank pages may be necessary when there is an 11x17 (foldout) figure or table because the foldout must begin on an odd-numbered page. The page after the foldout is also blank. Both blank pages are still counted in page numbering, however.

- Text font is 12 pt. Times, no bold.

- Standard practice for reports is full justification.

- Reports are usually printed on 8.5- x 11-inch white paper, single column.

- Report headings are usually 1.0, 1.1., 1.1.1, 1.1.1.1. Most companies prefer no number on heading levels 5, 6, etc. The figures below show the general and the outline number settings for Headings 1 and 2 in Microsoft Word (your preferred font type and size might be different than Arial 16 bold as I have for Heading 1, shown on Figure 6-2).

Figure 6-2   Heading 1 General Guidelines

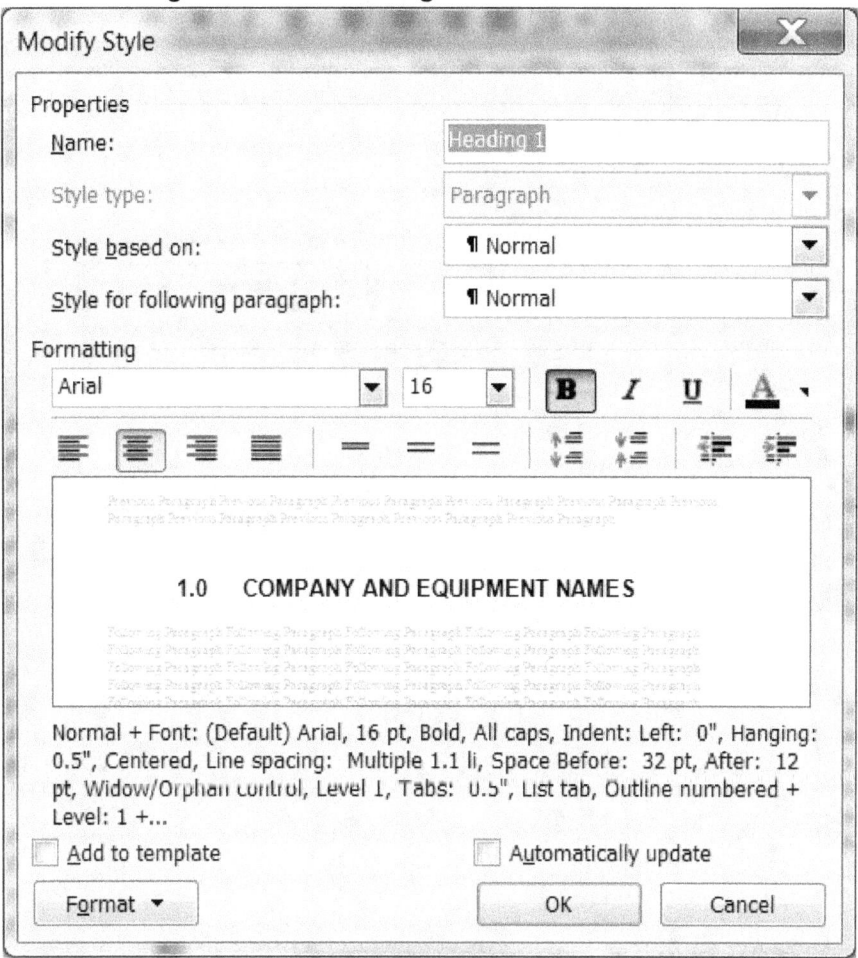

Figure 6-3   Heading 1 Outline Number Settings in Word

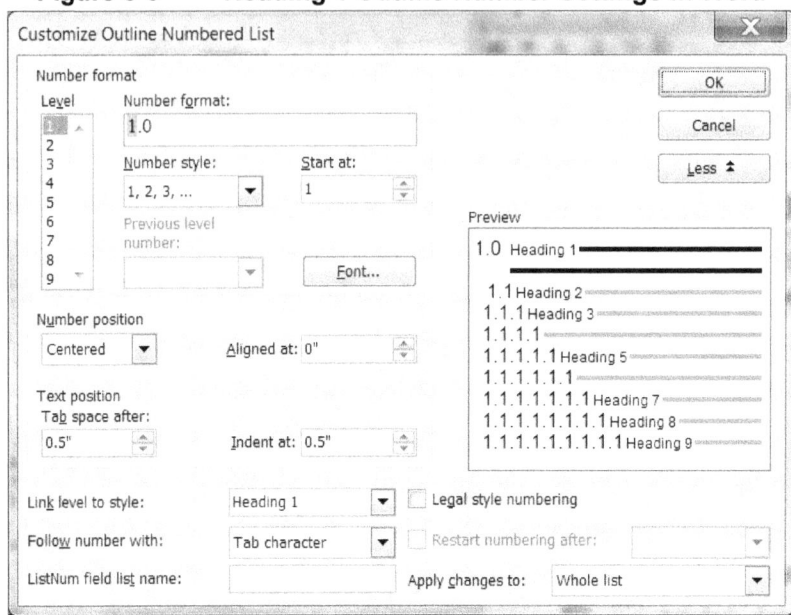

Figure 6-4   Heading 2 Outline Number Settings in Word

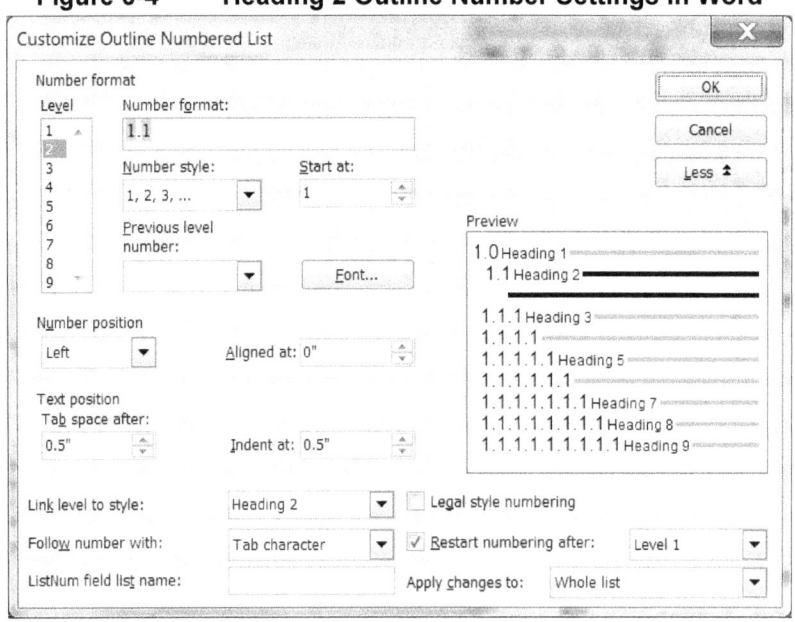

If you do not have a report template already, Wordsworth LLC (www.wordsworthwriting.net) sells report and proposal templates, as well as numerous other templates, with the heading and other styles already created and instructions inserted. The same documents, as well as thousands of government and business forms, can be purchased at Forms in Word (www.formsinword.com).

Figures and Tables

- Tables and figures are numbered according to the overall sections they are in. The second number has nothing to do with the subsections (second-, third-, and fourth-level headings); it is based on the table's order in that section. Therefore, Table 3-3 is the third table in Section 3 of the report.

- Capitalize the words *table* and *figure* only when they are used with a specific number (Table 4-4, the table).

- Use a hyphen, not a period, to separate table numbers (Table 5-7).

- Tables and figures appear after the first mention, either on the same page after the text mention or on the following page. They must be referred to in the text. Example: Figure 4-2, Site Location, identifies four areas of concern.

- Figure and table fonts are as follows: Arial 10, bold, centered. Then insert a tab before typing the title in title case (the reason for the tab instead of spaces is that it looks nicer in the Table of Contents). Table 6-1 and Figure 6-5 are examples.

Table 6-1   Cook Inlet Survey Data – 2002

Title Here – Bold and Centered	Title Here – 10 pt.	Title Here
Text in this column is usually left justified	Text in all other columns is usually centered	Text – All text is 10 pts.
Text	Text	Text
Text	Text	Text

Title Here – Bold and Centered	Title Here – 10 pt.	Title Here

Notes:

1. Always include definitions to all acronyms and notes below in smaller, indented font. Here I used 8 pt. font, Arial, no bold, left justified.
2. Note that the cells are merged here, and only the top border shows. Or you can include the notes below the table, and not within a cell.
3. Always "repeat" the header row, in case the table goes to a second page.

Key:

ADEC   Alaska Department of Environmental Conservation

USEPA   U.S. Environmental Protection Agency

Figure 6-5   Crevasse Moraine Trails

Notes:

1. I prefer to put figure captions above the figure, the same as table captions, so that I can have room for notes below a figure. I also prefer the look of the short figure captions that look nice in the Table of Contents.

2. Some companies prefer to add a third caption type, Photo, instead of using the word "Figure" for photographs.

3. I create a style called Table Notes that is smaller than the text and caption font and is set .2 spaces in, so that it is indented beneath the table. It has 2 points space before and 0 after. I use this same style for the blank paragraph under each figure and table (or after the last note if there are notes).

References

The format of references is a stylistic matter. There is no right or wrong (unless you are writing for a certain agency or company that has its own style guide). It may seem that there are almost as many reference styles as there are books. The main point is to be consistent—both throughout a document and throughout a company.

I prefer to base my references on *Chicago Manual of Style*, with some slight changes based on the hundreds of companies I have edited for. However, there are excellent online sources on Chicago Manual of style (such as this one for government citations at http://library.bowdoin.edu/help/chicago-gov.pdf or this one on general citations at http://www.chicagomanualofstyle.org/tools_citationguide.html), so Chicago might be a good one to follow). Within a month's time, I might use 10 different references styles, depending on what the client's needs are. Government agencies often have their own style guidelines; specific companies have their own style guides; academic writing has its own preferences [MLA, APA, etc.); newspapers and magazines might use AP or Chicago or their own guides). I believe the references sections is the most difficult part of a report because to find out what that particular company's preferences are and then to make all the entries (which can sometimes be in the hundreds) consistent are tricky. I also need (if the client understands the time involved in doing this correctly) to check every link to make sure it works and the spelling of titles and authors, as well as the dates, to be sure they are accurate.

My in-text citations usually just include the author (or agency) and the year. Whether or not to use a comma in between is again your choice, but be consistent; if the company has no preference, I leave out the commas, as in these examples: (Abrams 2012) (USFS 2014) (Coletta and Nagy 2014).

6.3.3.1.1 General Guidelines for References Section

Below are some overall guidelines to follow if your company does not have its own references style. The main point to keep in mind is to be consistent throughout your document. The main thing is to remember to be consistent. Your readers need to be able to find your references, if needed, so give them enough information to do so.

Entries should be alphabetically arranged by author's last name (first author listed in original text). If there is no author, list under the title. The order and description within entries are as follows:

1. Author(s) or editor(s). Spell out the names of authors and editors in the text as they appear on the title page of the document. Avoid using "et al." (which stands for "and others") in this list unless there are more than six authors' names; reserve et al. for the text when there are more than three authors.

2. Date. List the year of publication or "n.d." if there is no date available. If there are two or more reports by the same author in the same year, add a, b, c, etc. to the date in both text and list.

3. Title. Titles are typed in capital and lowercase letters (title case). Titles are either italicized, placed within quotation marks, or typed with no italics or quotation marks according to the following rules:

   — Books and reports. Italicize titles of all separate, freestanding, printed publications. Use standard capitalization rules, and spell out titles completely.

   — Journal articles, papers in proceedings, and manuscripts in collections. Titles of material contained within larger documents are put in quotation marks; the name of the larger work is italicized and spelled out in full.

   — Regulations and statutes. Titles of regulations and statutes are typed with no underline or quotation marks.

4. Editor, if entry by author.

5. Symposium or proceedings dates and locations in parentheses, if not part of the title.

6. Volume number.

7. Government or agency report number.

8. Mention of draft status, if applicable.

9. Revision or edition number.

10. Publisher.

11. Location of publisher (if a book). Use the two-letter U.S. Postal Service codes for state names. Publisher and location are not required when referencing a periodical (journal or magazine).

12. Page numbers (if an article). Insert the inclusive page numbers for articles within journals, proceedings, and technical reports,

preceded by "pp." if more than one page, or by "p." if only one page.

13. Month (and day, if available), if needed to distinguish between drafts, etc.

14. Web site accessed month, day, year: full link (if applicable).

6.3.4 Sample References Section

Note: These examples are in the style I use when a company has no preference; they aren't exactly *Chicago Manual of Style*, but close to it, and based on the list in Section 6.12.1 of this document.

Alaska Administrative Code. 2003. 5 AAC § 75.222 Policy for the Management of Sustainable Wild Trout Fisheries. Juneau, Alaska.

Alaska Department of Environmental Conservation (ADEC). 2012. *Alaska DEC User's Manual. Best Management Practices for Gravel/Rock Aggregate Extraction Projects: Protecting Surface Water and Groundwater Quality in Alaska.* Prepared by Shannon & Wilson, Inc. September. Web site accessed December 17, 2014: http://dec.alaska.gov/water/wnpspc/protection_restoration/bestm gmtpractices/Docs/GravelRockExtractionBMPManual.pdf.

Alaska Department of Fish and Game (ADF&G). 2014. Subsistence Regulations. Web site accessed August 14, 2013: http://www.adfg.alaska.gov/index.cfm?adfg=subsistenceregulati ons.main.

Alaska Energy Authority (AEA). 2012a. Renewable Energy Fund Round 6. Web site: http://www.akenergyauthority.org/RE_Fund-6.html. July.

Alaska Energy Authority (AEA). 2012b. Power Cost Equalization. Web site: http://www.akenergyauthority.org/programspce.html

Alaska Energy Authority (AEA). 2010. Alaska Energy Plan Community Database. Web site: http://www.akenergyauthority.org/alaska-energy-plan.html

Gill, A.B., and M. Bartlett. 2010. *Literature Review on the Potential Effects of Electromagnetic Fields and Subsea Noise From*

Marine Renewable Energy Developments on Atlantic Salmon, Sea Trout and European Eel. Scottish Natural Heritage Commissioned Report No. 401.

Institute of Social and Economic Research (ISER), University of Alaska Anchorage. 2012a. Internal Publications Database Search. Web site: http://www.iser.uaa.alaska.edu/publications.php?id=1518.

Institute of Social and Economic Research (ISER), University of Alaska Anchorage. 2012b. *Alaska Fuel Price Projections 2012-2035.* ISER Working Paper 2012.1 and Microsoft Excel Spreadsheet Price Model. July.

National Fire Protection Association. 2008. National Electrical Code. (NFPA70). Quincy, MA: National Fire Protection Association.

National Marine Fisheries Service (NMFS). 2013. *2013 Steller Sea Lion Protection Measures for Groundfish Fisheries in the Bering Sea and Aleutian Islands Management Area.* Preliminary Draft EIS/RIR/IRFA. March. Web site accessed August 13, 2013: http://www.npfmc.org/protected-species/steller-sea-lions/.

Person, D.K., and A.L. Russell. 2009. "Reproduction and Den Site Selection by Wolves in a Disturbed Landscape." *Northwest Science.* 83(3): pp. 211-24.

Person, D.K., M. Kirchhoff, V. Van Ballenberghe, G.C. Iverson, and E. Grossman. 1996. *The Alexander Archipelago Wolf: A Conservation Assessment.* USDA General Technical Report PNW-GTR-384.

Piatt, J.F., N.L. Naslund, and T.I. Van Pelt. 1999. "Discovery of a New Kittlitz's Murrelet Nest: Clues to Habitat Selection and Nest-Site Fidelity." *Northwestern Naturalist.* 80: pp. 8-13.

U.S. Fish and Wildlife Service. 1985. *Habitat Suitability Models and Instream Flow Suitability Curves: Chum Salmon,* by S.S. Hale, T.E. McMahon, and P.C. Nelson. Biological Report 82 (10, 108). August.

6.4　Proposals

Proposals are a marketing tool, and therefore we can have a bit more flexibility as far as formatting goes. In general, use the same formatting as the report. That can be fine for a proposal as well. If it is agreed to by the writer, editor, and project manager, such formatting changes such as columns, headings with color, text boxes featuring quotes from clients and advantages to using our company, and changes in fonts may be used. No more than two or possibly three (say, for tables) fonts should be used within one document.

6.5   Resumes

There are four standard resumes used by our company. Brief descriptions of these follow. As soon as you begin working here, you should write your resumes (in all four formats) and give them to the technical editor for editing and formatting. Also, if you already work for our company, you should update your resume at least every 6 months and give your changes to the technical editor.

6.5.1   *Resume: Standard Long Version*

- Treat each resume as a separate document. This means it should stand on its own, so all acronyms should be defined first use.

- Long resumes can be two or more pages.

6.5.2   *Resume: Short Version*

- Treat each resume as a separate document. This means it should stand on its own, so all acronyms should be defined first use.

- The short version is usually one page; two pages can be used if necessary.

6.5.3   *Resume: One Paragraph*

- These are used in proposals as well as on our Web site.

- Remember to update them frequently and give your changes to the technical editor.

6.5.4   *Resume: SF330 Form*

- For certain government proposals, we are required to use what is called the SF330 form. The font size is usually 10 points.

- There are certain standard sections to each SF330 form. (This form is available in Microsoft Word from www.formsinword.com.) A sample resume page from Forms in Word's/Wordsworth's "Sample SF330 Form Filled Out" is shown as Figure 6-6.

Figure 6-6   Sample SF330 Resume Page

E. RESUMES OF KEY PERSONNEL PROPOSED FOR THIS CONTRACT
(Complete one Section E for each key person.)

12. NAME	13. ROLE IN THIS CONTRACT	14. YEARS EXPERIENCE	
Darryl Rogain	Principal Architect & Quality Control	a. TOTAL 12	b. WITH CURRENT FIRM 7

15. FIRM NAME AND LOCATION *(City and State)*
ROGAIN DESIGN GROUP PC

16. EDUCATION *(DEGREE AND SPECIALIZATION)*	17. CURRENT PROFESSIONAL REGISTRATION *(STATE AND DISCIPLINE)*
• Bachelor of Architecture, University of Alaska • Participant – ATFP Workshop, Naval Facilities Engineering Service Center, 1999	• Architecture - Alaska #1874; Maryland #1232-A • Alaska #1235; Georgia #12864 • NCARB Certificate #43996

18. OTHER PROFESSIONAL QUALIFICATIONS *(Publications, Organizations, Training, Awards, etc.)*

19. RELEVANT PROJECTS

(1) TITLE AND LOCATION *(City and State)*	(2) YEAR COMPLETED	
Indefinite Quantity Contract for Architectural & Engineering Design Services for Various Projects, Army Base, Camp Lagoon, Alaska N62470-01-D-2002	PROFESSIONAL SERVICES 2003	CONSTRUCTION *(If applicable)* 2004

a. | (3) BRIEF DESCRIPTION *(Brief scope, size, cost, etc.)* AND SPECIFIC ROLE ☒ Check if project performed with current firm
Mr. Rogain was the principal architect and conducted quality control for numerous design/build projects at Camp Lagoon. Rogain Design Group provided design only on this project valued at $19.4 million. See Project #1 for complete details. Rogain's total cost was $1.2 million.

(1) TITLE AND LOCATION *(City and State)*	(2) YEAR COMPLETED	
IDIQ Contract for Architectural & Engineering Design Services for Various Projects, Army Base, Camp Lagoon, Alaska N62470-00-D-4751	PROFESSIONAL SERVICES 2002	CONSTRUCTION *(If applicable)*

b. | (3) BRIEF DESCRIPTION *(Brief scope, size, cost, etc.)* AND SPECIFIC ROLE ☒ Check if project performed with current firm
Mr. Rogain was the principal architect and conducted quality control for numerous design/build projects at Camp Lagoon. Complete A&E services were provided for projects totaling $3.9 million under this IDIQ contract. See Project #2 for complete details.

(1) TITLE AND LOCATION *(City and State)*	(2) YEAR COMPLETED	
IDIQ Contract for Architectural & Engineering Design Services for Various Projects, Army Base, Camp Lagoon, Alaska N62470-99-D-4087	PROFESSIONAL SERVICES 2001	CONSTRUCTION *(If applicable)*

c. | (3) BRIEF DESCRIPTION *(Brief scope, size, cost, etc.)* AND SPECIFIC ROLE ☒ Check if project performed with current firm
Mr. Rogain was the principal architect and conducted quality control for numerous design/build projects at Camp Lagoon. Complete A&E services were provided for projects totaling $7.56 million under this IDIQ contract. See Project #3 for complete details.

(1) TITLE AND LOCATION *(City and State)*	(2) YEAR COMPLETED	
IDIQ Contract for Architectural & Engineering Design Services for Various Projects at Army Base, Camp Lagoon, Alaska N62470-98-D-3895	PROFESSIONAL SERVICES 1999	CONSTRUCTION *(If applicable)*

d. | (3) BRIEF DESCRIPTION *(Brief scope, size, cost, etc.)* AND SPECIFIC ROLE ☒ Check if project performed with current firm
Mr. Rogain was the principal architect and conducted quality control for numerous design/build projects at Camp Lagoon. Complete A&E services were provided for projects totaling $10.92 million under this IDIQ contract. See Project #4 for complete details.

(1) TITLE AND LOCATION *(City and State)*	(2) YEAR COMPLETED	
IDIQ Contract for Architectural & Engineering Design Services for Various Projects, Army Base, Camp Lagoon, Alaska N62470-96-D-4486	PROFESSIONAL SERVICES 1999	CONSTRUCTION *(If applicable)*

e. | (3) BRIEF DESCRIPTION *(Brief scope, size, cost, etc.)* AND SPECIFIC ROLE ☐ Check if project performed with current firm
Mr. Rogain was the principal architect and conducted quality control for numerous design/build projects at Camp Lagoon. Complete A&E services were provided for projects totaling $6.074 million under this IDIQ contract. See Project #5 for complete details.

7.0   USING THE REVIEWING FEATURES IN MICROSOFT WORD

To start, I make sure I change my document template or the Word file I am using so that my Track Changes Options look like the ones on Figures 7-1 and 7-2:

- Word 2003: Under Tools, Options, Track Changes, the selections should look exactly like on Figure 7-1

- Word 2007 and later: Under Review, Track Changes, Change Tracking Options, make your selections match Figure 7-2.

Since the default has some oddities, you might not see the edits correctly if you do not change your settings to what I have shown on Figure 7-1 (or Figure 7-2 for Word 2007).

Also, be sure you always use View, Print Layout when you view texts. Word 2003 by default opens in Reading Layout, which is not the best way to work or see edits, in my view (in fact, you can easily disable it in Tools, Options, General, by unclicking "Allow starting in Reading Layout").

Figure 7-1   Track Changes Options in Microsoft Word 2003

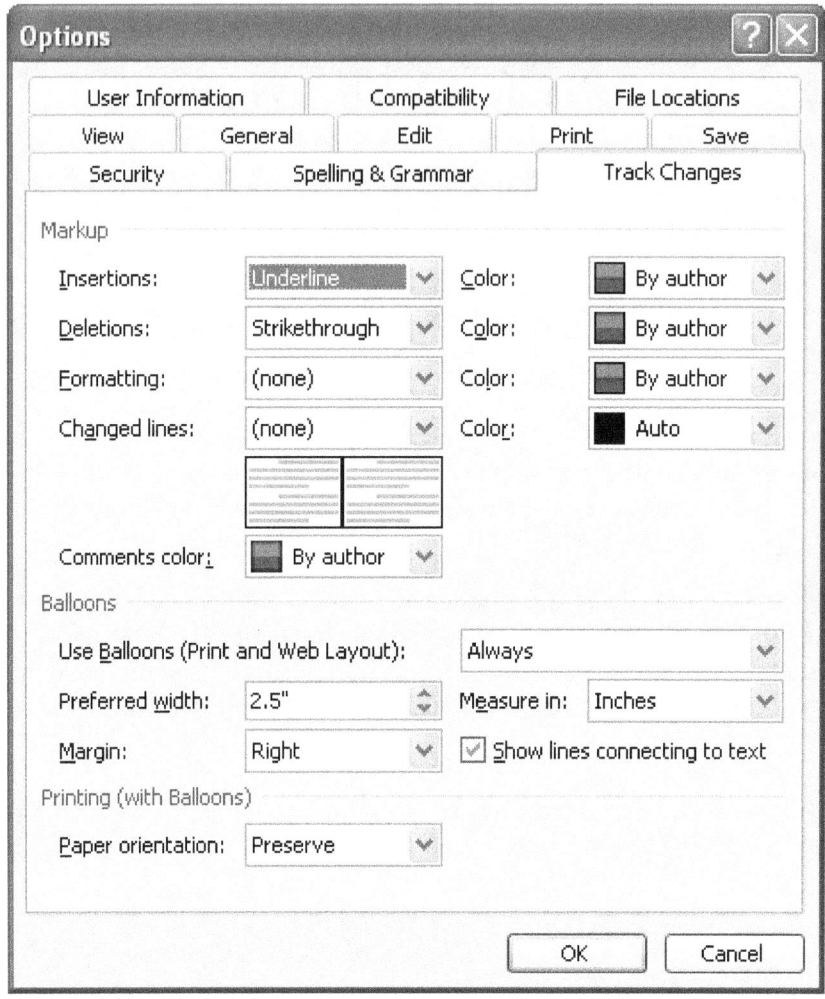

Figure 7-2   Track Changes Options in Microsoft Word 2007

Track Changes Options					? X
Markup					
Insertions:	Color only	▼	Color:	■	Dark Red ▼
Deletions:	Strikethrough	▼	Color:	■	Dark Red ▼
Changed lines:	(none)	▼	Color:	■	Dark Red ▼
Comments:	■ By author	▼			
Moves					
☑ Track moves					
Moved from:	Double strikethrough	▼	Color:	■	Green ▼
Moved to:	Double underline	▼	Color:	■	Green ▼
Table cell highlighting					
Inserted cells:	■ Light Blue	▼	Merged cells:	□	Light Yellow ▼
Deleted cells:	■ Pink	▼	Split cells:	□	Light Orange ▼
Formatting					
☑ Track formatting					
Formatting:	(none)	▼	Color:	■	By author ▼
Balloons					
Use Balloons (Print and Web Layout):			Always		▼
Preferred width:	3"	▲▼	Measure in:	Inches	▼
Margin:	Right	▼			
☐ Show lines connecting to text					
Paper orientation in printing:			Preserve		▼
				OK	Cancel

7.1   Using Track Changes

"Track Changes" is a feature of Word that allows each user to view comments and revisions throughout the review process. Once enabled, Word will automatically track each change you make in the document. It will also use different colors for different authors and editors (to a point). Figure 7-3 shows a major rewrite of Web site text using track changes. Deletions and comments are shown in the right margin while the main editor's changes are in blue; a second editor's changes are in red.

Figure 7-3   Example from a Web Sited Edited with Track Changes and Comments

7.1.1   Using the Reviewing Toolbar

To see the reviewing toolbar, go to View, Toolbars, and be sure Reviewing is checked (see Figure 7-4).

Figure 7-4 How to Add the Reviewing Toolbar

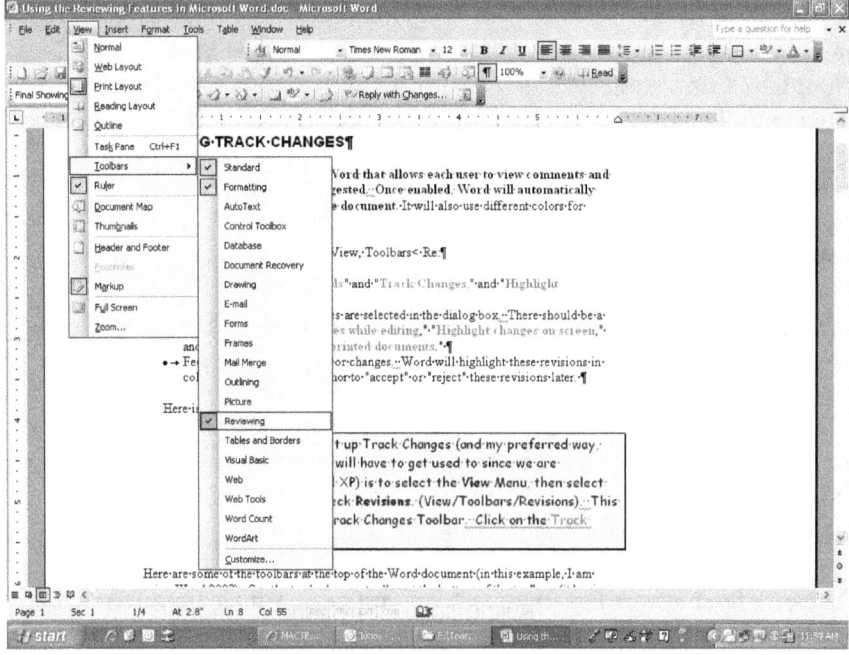

Figure 7-5 lists some of the toolbars at the top of a Word 2003 document. See the track changes toolbar at the bottom of the toolbars (it begins with "Final Showing Markup" indented from the left, then "Show."

Figure 7-5 Microsoft Word Toolbars

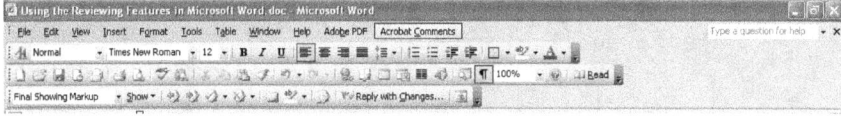

The bottom toolbar is the Reviewing toolbar. To the right of "Show" are the yellow boxes with blue arrows that show you how to go from comment to comment, the yellow box with the blue checkmark that allows you to accept a change or comment (or all comments if you select the dropdown arrow next to it), and the red X that allows you to delete a comment (or all comments if you select the dropdown).

7.1.2 *Accepting All Changes*

Important: to the right of the yellow box with the **blue checkmark** is a **small black down arrow**. Click on this to open a feature that allows you to **accept all changes in a document**. Generally, this is what you want to do once you have glanced through the editor's changes—accept all changes. (Most editors use track changes for changes they are sure of, such as mechanics and style issues. They use the "insert comments" feature for doubts.)

Note: At certain companies, to prevent the writers from having to spend too much time reviewing edits, the editor will not use track changes for the edits she is sure about such as style, grammar, punctuation, etc. This way the writer will not be distracted and will only have to look for the comments (or areas with track changes where the editor was not 100% certain of the changes). Let the editor know if you prefer to see all changes; this is up to the writer.

Then, use the blue arrows to go to the **comments,** which are different from the track changes. (You might prefer to go through and see the comments first, before accepting all changes, in case the editor has inserted comments such as "change ok?" So that you can clearly see through the track changes what the change was.)

When you receive your file back, you can either accept or reject the changes. You can read comments three ways:

1.   By hovering your mouse cursor over the highlighted text if the "balloons" are not on.

2.   By looking at the comments in the comment box in the right-hand margin (if the balloons are on, which they are in this document) (see Figure 7-6).

3.   By looking at the comments bar at the bottom of your screen (see Figure 7-7).

Figure 7-6   Comment in Right Margin

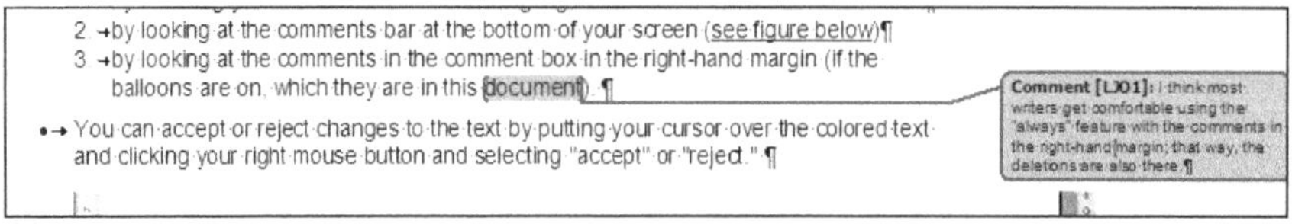

You can accept or reject changes to the text by putting your cursor over the colored text and clicking your right mouse button and selecting "accept" or "reject." You can delete the comment by clicking in the comment and then selecting the red X to delete it in the track changes toolbar.

Figure 7-7 shows how comments will be listed below the text (at the bottom of your screen) if you turn off balloons in the track changes options menu.

Figure 7-7   Comments Showing Below Document Instead of Margin

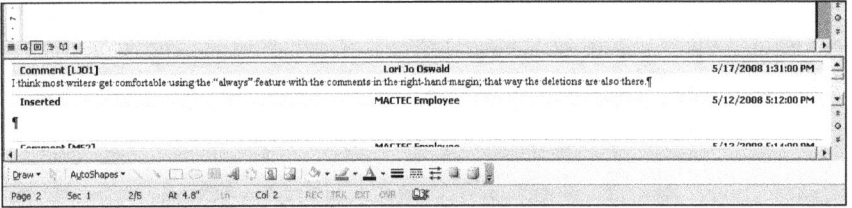

7.2   Accepting Certain Changes in Word

It might be helpful for authors to know how to accept certain changes only, so they know how to accept just my edits or formatting changes and still see the other reviewers' changes in tracked changes.

7.2.1   How to Accept Formatting Changes Only

Click the arrow to the right of Show on your reviewing toolbar (see Section 7.1.1 if you are not sure what the reviewing toolbar is), deselect everything but Formatting. Then click the arrow beside Accept Change and select Accept All Changes Shown. (Or you can hide them by just clearing Formatting from the Show menu.)

7.2.2   How to Accept Changes by One Person

Do the same process (as in Section 7.2.1) to show the edits by one person. Go to show, then reviewers, unclick all reviewers, and then just click on the ones you want to see and accept (such as Lori Jo Oswald and Eva Nagy for the technical editing). Then accept all changes shown.

7.2.3   How to Turn on Balloon Layout for Comments

Figure 7-8 is an example of two balloon comments, one from Lori Jo
(LJO1 = Lori Jo's first comment in the document), and one from an
editor with ME for initials (ME2 = ME second comment in the
document).

Figure 7-8   Balloons in Word Showing Two Commenters

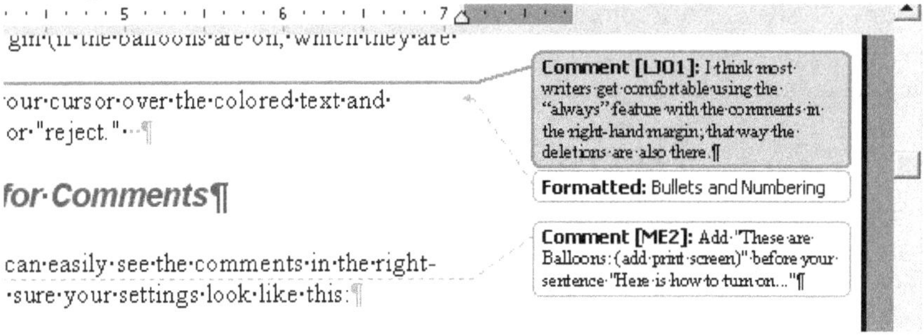

Figure 7-9 shows how to turn on the "balloons" layout option so that you
can easily see the comments in the right-hand margin. Go to Tools,
Options, Track Changes. Then make sure your settings look like this:

Figure 7-9   Turning on Balloons Layout

7.3   Using Comments

7.3.1   Comments Overview

The inserted comments are where the editor had some doubt, question, or requested more information. This is where you will want to either respond or ignore the comment, and then delete each comment (using the red "x" as described next).

To the right of the small down arrow is the yellow box with the **red "x" that allows you to delete a change or comment**. To the right of the red "x" is the yellow box that allows you to **insert comments**, and to the right of that is the **redlined track changes** box that allows you to turn on or off the track changes feature. Figure 7-5 shows the track changes toolbar from Word 2003. (In Word 2007 and later, just click the Review ribbon.)

In general, once you have the toolbar open on your screen, just click on the redlined "track changes" icon on the reviewing toolbar to begin inserting changes.

7.3.2   How to Attach Your Name to the Comments

- Since there may be several editors or reviewers inserting comments, it is important to attach your name to your comments in case the author has questions.
- To attach your name, go to "Tools" and select "Options." Choose "User Information" and fill in your name and your initials (see Figure 7-10). You will only have to do this once on your computer, but if you change computers, you will need to do it again.

Figure 7-10   Adding Your Name and Initials to Word Documents

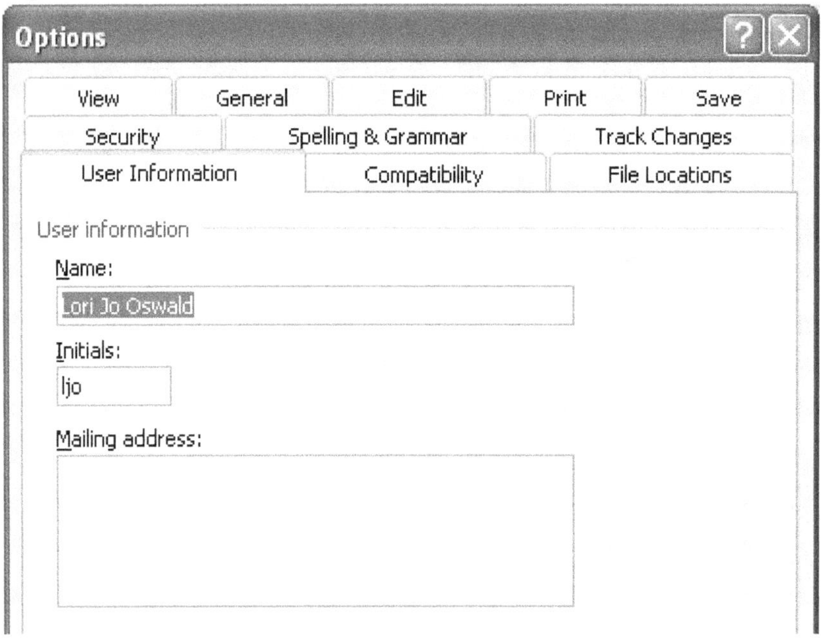

7.4　Preparing the Document for Reviewing

Make sure that you have the "Reviewing" toolbar selected so that it shows up in your toolbar. If it is not there, go to "View" and select "toolbars" and "reviewing."

To begin making comments, click on the "track changes" icon on the reviewing toolbar.

7.5　Reviewing the Document

You can now change the text directly in the document by typing or deleting and your changes will appear in color.

You can also insert a comment or question to the author by highlighting the text in question and clicking on the "Insert Comment" icon. This brings up a comment box for you to insert questions or comments.

When you actually have a comment to insert, use the yellow box (with no red or blue arrows or "x's" in it). Click the yellow box, and a comment box will be inserted at whatever point your cursor is in the text. Just type in your comment, and then click your mouse in the text to continue). Figure 7-11 is an example of a comment inserted into Word 2003:

Figure 7-11　　Comment Example

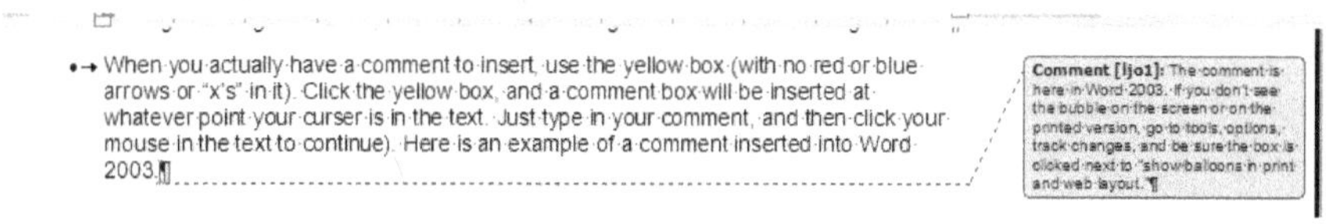

Additional Information

Below is a link to a Microsoft Word training program that covers using Track Changes in Word 2003; you can Google "free training track changes in Word 2007" or whatever version you are using to find one specific to your version.
http://office.microsoft.com/training/training.aspx?AssetID=RC01160013 1033

8.0 FORMATTING AND WRITING TABLES

As with any company style, the main thing to remember with tables is to be consistent in your format. This section provides tips for formatting tables, but you might prefer a different format or shading. Still, by reading this chapter, you will understand how to make a table in Microsoft Word, and you can apply this knowledge to your own format.

8.1 Captions

The captions, or titles, of tables should be as follows:

Table 1   Title Here in Upper and Lower Case

Note the features of the above:

1. Arial 10 point bold.

2. Title in standard title case: upper and lower case.

3. Space after table title is 3 points, to separate it slightly from the table title.

4. There is no period at the end of either the table number line or the table title line.

Note that if section numbering is included instead of the 1, 2, 3, 4 format, the table and figure numbers will be different than the above example, as shown below:

Table 1-1   Title Here

Table 1-2   Title Here

Table 1-3a   Title Here

Table 1-3b   Title Here

8.2 Table Numbering

The numbering of the tables and figures should be consistent throughout the document and will depend on the numbering used in the main document.

8.2.1 Alphanumeric Numbering System

Some government agencies prefer alphanumeric numbering (I.A, I.A.1, I.A.1.a., etc.); in this case, the numbering of the table starts with the main section number where it is first mentioned in the text, followed by a period, followed by the section letter where it is first mentioned in the text (i.e., Table II.A), followed by the table number (determined by the order of the tables). Here are some examples:

- II.A-1, II.A.2, II.A-3

- III.C-1, III-C-2

The writer or editor might also choose to number related tables with an additional small letter, as follows: IV.1-9a, IV.1-9b, IV.1-9c

8.2.2 Numeric Numbering System

For the more traditional numbering system, which uses numbering only (i.e., 1.0, 1.1, 1.1.1, 1.1.1.1), the tables and figures are numbered by the section that they appear in followed by a hyphen, followed by the number (which is determined by order). Here, as an example, are the first five table numbers from Section 2.0 of a report:

Table 2-1

Table 2-2

Table 2-3

Table 2-4

Table 2-5

Note that for this method, the table (and figure) numbers only use two levels of numbering; it does not make a difference whether the tables appear in a first-, second-, third-, or fourth-level heading. They are still numbered in order of their textual reference. Also, no roman numerals are used. (As an example, this document uses this method for numbering sections and tables.)

8.3   Table Borders

8.3.1   Standard Borders

For most company tables, we use ½ point borders inside and outside. Some agencies or clients prefer thick borders on the outside as well as under the header row in tables:

1. For the outside border, as well as the border around the outside of the table header row(s), we use a 1½ point black border (or line).

2. For the inside of the table, we use a ¾-line border. Borders will be used around all items within a table for consistency and readability.

Table 8-1 is an example of our main borders.

Table 8-1   Standard Borders

8.3.2   Special Column Borders

A bolder line (1½ points) may be used between columns in one case: when there are multiple cells within a column, as in the following example (Table 8-2).

Table 8-2   Table Showing Bold Borders within Table Columns

		Title Here (Days)			Title Here (Days)			Title Here (Days)		
Title Here	**Title Here**	10	20	30	10	20	30	10	20	30

8.3.3   Special Row Borders

The heavier border (1-1/2 points) may be used between rows in one case—when subtitle rows are included (subtitle rows are described in Section 8.4.2 of this document). Note that in such a case, only the row above the subtitle row has the thicker border. See Table 8-3 for an example.

Table 8-3   Table Showing Bold Border within Table Rows

Title Here	Title Here	Title Here	Title Here	Title Here
Subtitle Here				
Subtitle Here				
Subtitle Here				

8.4   Table Shading

We use shading in several ways and in several percentages, based on the area of the table the shaded areas are in, as described below:

8.4.1   Header Rows

The main use of the heading, and probably the only use for most tables, is in the header row. This is the first (top) row of the table, which sometimes includes several cells within a column. This entire area will be shaded at 15%. Table 8-4 is an example.

Table 8-4   Header Row Shading

Table 8-5 is another example, with multiple cells within a column.

Table 8-5   Multiple Cell Shading

Title Here[1]	Title Here[2]	Title Here (Days)			Title Here (Days)			Title Here (Days)		
		10	20	30	10	20	30	10	20	30

Notes:

[1] Note that the cell alignment for the far left top row is left justified, bottom of row.

[2] Note that the cell alignment for the rest of the header rows is centered, bottom of row.

8.4.2   Shaded Rows within Table Body

This section describes the two ways shading is used within a table body: for subtitle rows and long data tables.

Subtitle Rows

For tables with subtitles (i.e., subheadings) within the table body, do the following:

1. Merge the cells for the subtitle row.

2. Use Arial 10 point bold for the subtitle font.

3. Left justify the subtitle.

4. Use 10% shading for the entire row where the subtitle is.

5. Use the bolder line (1½ points) for the border above the subtitle row.

6. The paragraph spacing is 2 points above and below the text for the subtitle row, the same as the rest of the table body and header rows.

See Table 8-6 for an example.

Table 8-6   Subtitle Row Shading

Title Here	Title Here	Title Here	Title Here	Title Here
Subtitle Here				
Subtitle Here				
Subtitle Here				

8.4.3   Data Tables Longer Than One Page

For lengthy data tables (more than one page) with no subtitles, use alternating shaded lines to separate data lines from each other, as in the following example (Table 8-7). Note that the alternate shaded lines use 5% shading, but if this does not show when printed, use 10%.

Table 8-7   Shading for Data Tables Longer Than One Page

For consistency and readability, no shading should be used except for those three reasons described above.

8.5   Table Text

Table text, generally, should have the following features:

- Font—Arial, 10 points, centered, not bolded, not italicized

- Width—Table width is across the page. Margins for table and figure pages are 1 inch from top and bottom, and 1.5 inches from left and right.

- Paragraph Spacing—Table text is single space, with a 2-point space above and below the text.

- Justification—Most table text is centered, but here are exceptions:

  - Often the left-hand column and header will be left justified.

  - In addition, if numbers or figures (money) with decimal places are used, the columns will be right justified, allowing just enough space from the right cell border to look balanced within the columns.

- Blank Cells—There should never be a "blank cell." Use either NA or -- to fill each cell where no data are listed. See Table 8-8 for an example.

- Cell Alignment—For the header row, align the cells at the bottom (in Microsoft Word, select the header row, right click, choose cell alignment, and choose the bottom centered tab). All rows are centered except, in some cases, the left row, which would be left justified (including the header).

- Note that no italics or all-capitalized words (except acronyms and abbreviations) are used in the table body (see Table 8-8).

Table 8-8   Sample "Blank Cell" Data and Notes

		--	NA	

Notes:

-- = No data are available for this sample.

NA = Not applicable.

A table font style with these features will be set up in the report and proposal templates for use by data processors, editors, and writers.

Exceptions: The table font size and table width can vary depending on need and text (see Section 8.6 for a discussion of table width). If, for example, it is possible to fit a table onto one page if the font size is changed to 9 points and the notes (as discussed in Section 8.7) are reduced to 8 point, the document processor has that freedom. Similarly, if the document processor needs to make the paragraph spacing above and below the table text 1 point instead of 2 to fit the table to one page, that is acceptable.

8.6 Table Width and Justification

In general, the table width is across the page.

Margins for table and figure pages are 1" from top and bottom, and 1.5" from left and right.

Exception: It is acceptable for narrow tables (for example, 2 to 3 columns with little text) to not use the entire page width. In that case, just narrow the column width to a bit wider than the text. See Table 8-9 for an example.

Table 8-9   Exception to Page Width for Tables

8.7 Table Notes

Table notes can come with three headings: Notes, Key, and Source, and if more than one is used, they should appear in that order.

Table notes have the following features:

- Arial, 9 point

- The first word (such as "Notes:" in Table 8-10, below) should have a 3-point space between it and the bottom border of the table.

- Left justified

- The words "Key:" "Notes:" and "Source:" will be bold (the colon is also bold).

- There is no border around the table notes section (see Table 8-10).

- Footnotes are included under the "Notes" heading.

- "Key" is used when acronyms and abbreviations need to be defined; the format is shown in Table 8-10.

- The words "Notes:" "Key:" and "Source:" appear on a separate line from the text that follows, as shown in Table 8-10.

- Periods are used for complete sentences and source listings.

- For acronym and abbreviation listings, no periods are used. An equal (=) sign is used between the acronym and the definition, as in GRO = gasoline range organics.

- Follow regular capitalization rules when defining acronyms and abbreviations. If the definition is capitalized (for example, EPA = Environmental Protection Agency), capitalize it in the Key section. If the definition is not usually capitalized (for example, PAH = polycyclic aromatic hydrocarbons), do not capitalize it in the Key section. (See Table 8-10.)

- Note that some clients prefer an equal sign (=) or an en dash with spaces between the abbreviation and the definition in the table notes (see Table 8-10). Personally, I prefer tabs, so if the company does not have its own style guide, I use tabs, as follows:

  USFWS   U.S. Forest Service

Table 8-10   Table Notes, Key, and Sources Example

Title Here	Title Here	Title Here (Days)	Title Here (Days)	Title Here (Days)
		23^1		
		45		
		62		

Notes:

Production and reserve data as of December 2000.

[1] Days estimated based on results from November 2001 sampling.

Key:

DRO = diesel range organics

EPA = Environmental Protection Agency

Source:

Griffiths and Gallaway (1982).

9.0 COMMONLY USED WORDS

The purpose of this section is to provide consistency with certain words.
Is it one word or two? Is there a hyphen or not? Should it be capitalized
or not? When in doubt, use *Merriam-Webster's Collegiate Dictionary* to
be sure. Here are some examples from one company's documents:

- as-built (when used as an adjective preceding a noun, as in as-
  built survey)
- echo sounder (two words, Webster's)
- echo sounding (not in Webster's, but presumably two words
  based on echo sounder)
- fieldwork
- side-scan sonar (hyphen and use with the word sonar, Webster's)
- site-specific (adjective preceding noun)
- static GPS
- subbottom (not sub-bottom)

As you come across words that you think need to be included in this list
(or changed), suggest them to the technical editor for future editions of
this style guide.

Note: The words below are based on our client's preferences, Webster's,
and government agency preferences, but your company may prefer a
different spelling. If a word is not found in Webster's (www.m-w.com)
as one word (such as streambank, which is listed here as one word
because many clients prefer it that way; however, if the company does
not have a preference, I will make it two words since it does appear in
Webster's as one [i.e., stream bank]). But company style rules.
Therefore, you may have your own preferences for some of these.
Examples are wellfield (*well field* since not in dictionary, but often one
word per company preference) and *work plan* (two words since not in
Webster's, but many companies prefer workplan).

Note: Adjectives listed with hyphens only take the hyphen when they
appear *before* the noun.

A

above grade (adverb: occurred above grade)

above ground (adverb: occurred 50 feet above ground)

abovegrade (adjective: before noun; abovegrade work)

aboveground (adjective: aboveground tank, but: pipe was located above ground)

absorption

accommodate

acrolein

across-bed

adapter (not adaptor)

adsorb (vs. absorb)

adsorption

aerial

air bag (noun)

air conditioning (noun)

airborne

air-cooled

airflow

airport

airstream

airtight

all right (incorrect: alright)

allocable

alluvial, alluvium

already, all ready

analog (a chemical compound that is structurally similar to another); otherwise, use analogue

analytes

anemometer

anion

anisotropy, anis tropic

anticline

appendices (plural)

appendix (singular)

aquifer, aquitard

areal

areawide

auger

autoignition

autorefrigeration

autotransformer

B

back draft

back pressure (not back-pressure unless adjective before noun)

back up (verb)

backfill (noun), backfilled

backflow

backhoe

backlighted

backup (noun, adjective)

backwash

backwater

back welding

backyard

baffle board

baghouse

bakehouse

bar screen

bark chips

bark dust

base flow

base map

base station

baseline

base-neutral-acid

baseplate

bases (plural of basis)

basewide

basinwide

bathymetric (adjective)
bathymetrical (adjective)
bathymetrically (adverb)
bathymetry (noun)
bay water
bedrock
behavior (not behaviour)
below grade (adverb: occurred below grade)
below ground (adverb: occurred below the ground)
below-grade (adjective or noun)
belowground (adjective: belowground sampling)
bench mark (permanent elevation marker)
benchlands
benchmark (standard; point of reference)
bench-scale
biannual (occurring twice a year)
biennial (occurring every 2 years)
biocell
biodegradeable
bioremediation
bioturbated
bioventing
biweekly
block work (construction)
blow line
blow-count (noun)
blowdown (noun, adjective)
blow down (verb)
blowup (noun, adjective); blow up (verb)
bondholder
bookkeeping
borehole

bottom-land
bottommost
break down (verb)
breakdown (noun)
breakup (noun)
build out (verb)
build up (verb)
buildout (noun)
build-up (adjective)
buildup (noun)
built-up
bulldozer
buoys
buy back (verb)
buy-back (adjective: buy-back terms)
bypass
by-product

C

caliper (not calliper)
campground
canary grass
canister (Webster's prefers to cannister)
cannot
carbureted
carryover
casthouse
cataclastic
catch basin
cation
Cenozoic era
center pivot
centerline
centigrade (international term for Celsius)
chain wheel
chain-link (adjective: chain-link fence)

chain-of-custody (adjective)
change-out
Charpy
check out (verb)
check stop
checklist
checkout (noun)
checkpoint
chipboard
citywide
clayey
claypan
claystone
clean up (verb)
cleanup (adjective/noun;
cleanup equipment)
climatological
close out (verb)
closeout (adjective/noun)
close-up
coal tar
coarse-grained (adjective)
coastline
coauthor
cobbly
cocaptain
cochair
co-composting
co-containment
cofferdam
colinear
colluvium
color (not colour)
combined-sewer (adjective)
commingle
companywide
compatibility
condenser (not condensor)
connate

constant-discharge test
contaminant (noun)
contaminate (verb)
conterminous
cool down
co-own
co-owner
co-ownership
corehole
Coriolis (effect or force)
corrosion-resistant (adjective)
cost-effective (adjective)
cost-effectiveness
cost-of-service (adjective: cost-of-service fees)
coulomb
Coulomb field
Coulomb force
counter-rotate
countertop
court-ordered (adjective)
coworker
cowrite
crop out (verb)
cropland
cross connection
cross contamination
cross over (verb)
cross section
cross ties (noun)
cross-checking
crosscut
crossgradient
crossover (noun)
cross-reference
cross-sectional
curbside
cutoff (adjective: cutoff date)
cutout

D

dam site
data (plural), datum (singular)
data sets
database
datalogger
datum (singular)
dead leg
decahydration
decision maker
decision making (noun)
decision-making (adjective)
de-emphasize
deenergize
deice
deionized
-demand (peak-demand period)
-density (high-density protein)
desiccate
DEW Line
dew point
dewatered
dialogue (Webster's prefers to dialog)
dielectric
digester
dilatancy
DoD (lowercase "o")
DOE (uppercase "O")
double up
downdip
downdropping (adjective: downdropping slope)
downgradient
downhill
downhole
downslope
downspout
downstream (adjective or adverb)
downtime
drain field
drain line
drainageway
drain-down (adjective)
drainpipe
draw down (verb)
drawdown (noun)
drill bit
drill head
drill hole
drill rig
drip pan
drip-proof
drivetrain (one word if referring to automobiles; otherwise, two words)
drive-train components
drop box (noun)
drop off (verb)
drop-box (adjective: drop-box service)
drop-off (adjective: drop-off items)
dry cleaning (noun), dry-clean (verb)
dry wall
dry well
dual-phase extraction
ductwork
dump truck
dunnage
dust tight

E

earth flow
earth moving equipment
earthfill
earthwork

east side
easternmost (but east side)
echo sounder
echo sounding
ecotoxicity
ecotoxicological
electro (no hyphen or space; combine with next word, as in:)
electrohydraulic
electromelt
E-logs
e-mail
embayment
end caps (noun)
end point
end product
end result
end seal
ensure
errata
erratum
Ethernet
evapotranspiration
ex situ (no hyphen or italics)
exceedance (not exceedence)
-exempt (tax-exempt bond)
explosionproof
extra-capacity (adjective: extra-capacity trunks)
Extranet

F
facies (noun singular and plural)
fail-safe (adjective/noun)
falling-head test
fallout
farmland
fast track (noun)
fast-track (adjective)
fatal-flaw (adjective: fatal-flaw

analysis)
feasibility
federal
-feed (center-feed clarifier; step-feed mode)
feed line
feed well
feedstock
feedwater
fence line
fence post
fiberglass
field crew
field screening techniques
field streaming
field worker
fieldbus
field-wide
fieldwork (noun)
fine-grained (adjective)
fine-tune
fire chief
fire control
fire department
fire drill
fire escape
fire extinguisher
fire fighting (noun)
fire pump
fire screen
fire station
fire truck
firebox
firedamp
firefighter, fireman
fire-fighting (adjective)
firefighting (verb)
firehouse
fireman

fireplug
fireproof
firesafe
firewall
firewater
firework
firmwide
fish (for plural)
fish screen
fishkill
flame ionization
flare up (verb)
flareup (adjective/noun)
flash point
flip chart
flood way
floodplain
floodwater
floor plate
floppy disk
-flow (restricted-flow issues; on-flow train)
flow line
flow path
flow rate
flow sheet
flow stream
flow top
flowchart
flowmeter
fluoride
fluvial
fly ash
-focus (deep-focus earthquake)
focused (not focussed)
follow up (verb)
follow-up (noun/adjective)
food chain
force main

forego
foregoing
forklift
formwork (construction)
fossiliferous (adjective)
freestanding
freezeback
Freon
fresh water (noun)
freshwater (adjective)
friable
front loader
front yard
front-end loader
fulfill (not fulfil)
full time (noun)
full-time (adjective: full-time equivalent)
furans
fuse holder
FY 99, FY 00

G

gas station
gas-oil (mixture)
gauge (not gage)
gauge line
gauss
gearbox
geochemical
geodetic
geologic (except U.S. Geological Survey)
geomembrane
geomorphic
Geo-probe
geotechnical
geotextile
giveaway
-glass (cast-glass ceramics)

glass-ceramic (noun and
adjective)
gneissic
-grade (at-grade floor)
-graded (well-graded roadway)
grain-size analysis
grassland
grasslike
gray (not grey)
green chain
-grid (coarse-grid receptor)
gridded
ground bed
ground cover
groundwater (except National
Ground Water Association) (but
note: surface water)

H
half-life (noun)
halocarbons
halogen
hand out (verb)
hand switch
handheld
handhold
handhole
handout (noun)
hands-on
hard copy
hard hat
head loss
head shaft
headspace
headwall
headworks
heterogeneity
high resistivity (adjective)
high-capacity production
high-level (adjective)

hillslope
HNu (brand name, portable)
hold-down (tanks)
holding time (not hold time)
holdup (delay)
hollow-stem (adjective)
Holocene
homeowner
homogeneous, homogeneity
hook hole
hookup
horsepower
hot spot
hydro (note: no hyphen after
hydro)
hydrogeology, hydrogeologic
hydropower
HydroPunch (but lowercase if
generic)
hydrotest

I
ice floes
in depth (adverb: studied in
depth)
in situ (no hyphen or italics)
inboard (adjective)
in-board (adjective: in-board
motor)
incompatibility
in-county (adjective: in-county
use)
in-depth (adjective: in-depth
evaluation)
inflow (noun)
inhomogeneous
in-house (adjective: in-house
distribution)
in-line (adjective: in-line
service)

in-place (adjective: in-place test)

in-plant (adjective: in-plant operations)

in-service (adjective: in-service testing)

installation-wide

in-stream

interbred, interbredded

interdisciplinary

interfinger

interlayered

intermittent

intermodular

Internet

ion exchange

isoctane

isotropic

iterative

J
job site

judgment

juxtapose

K
Kelvin

kerosine (component of jet fuel)

keylock

kick off (verb)

kickoff (noun)

Kjeldahl

kriging

L
label, labeled, labeling

lamina (noun singular), laminae (plural)

land clearing

landfarm

landfill (noun)

landform

landowner

landslide

land-spreading (adjective)

land-take (adjective as in land-take requirements)

large-scale

lay-up

leach field

leach line

leachate

leak-proof

leak-tight

least squares (noun plural)

leftover

-level (low-level radiation)

life cycle (noun)

life raft

life span

life-cycle (adjective preceding noun)

lignin

-like (only if preceded by double 11:likelihood

line pipe

line shaft

lineal

linear

liquefaction

lithologic (adjective)

load out (verb)

-loading (barge-loading facility)

load-out (adjective)

lockdown

lockset

logbook

lognormal (adjective)

long range (noun)

long term (adverb/noun)

long-range (adjective)
long-standing
long-term (adjective)
low-capacity tank
lowlands
low-lying (adjective)
low-permeability (adjective)
low-resistivity (adjective)
low-yield
lunch room
lysimeter

M
main line
mainframe
make up (verb)
makeup (noun and adjective)
-making (steel-making process)
man-day (use workday)
manganese
manlift
man-made
maplet
medium (noun singular), media (noun plural)
medium-grained (adjective)
medium-range missile
medium-sized
megascopic
meltwater
mesic
metasediments
meter (not metre)
Method Three (not Method 3)
micaceous (adjective)
microcomputer
micromho(s)
microorganism
microwell
midpoint

milestone
mill water
millscale
minimize (not minimise)
modeling (not modelling)
moistureproof
monitoring well
mudflow
multi (no hyphen; join with next word)
multibeam
multidisciplinary
multifamily residence
multilayered
multimedia
multipathway
multiphase
multitask
multiyear

N
nameplate
naphtha
nationwide
no-action (adjective: no-action alternative)
no-build (adjective: no-build alternative)
nonconductive
non-debt-funded (adjective: non-debt-funded project)
nondetect
nonequilibrium
nonhazardous
nonlisted
nonmarine
nonroutine
non-steady-state (adjective: non-steady-state issues)
nontoxic

nonturbid
nonvolatile
non-water-bearing
nonwettable
northernmost
northwest-southeast
northwest-trending
N-value (noun)

O

obturator
occur/occurred/occurrence
off-gas
off-line
off-load
off-loading
off-peak (adjective)
off-post or off post
off-road (adjective: off-road vehicle)
offset (noun, adjective, or verb)
offshore
off-site (adjective and adverb)
off-take (point)
oil field
oil rig
oil well
oilless
on line (in or into operation)
ongoing
on-line (adjective or adverb)
on-post or on post
onshore
on-site (adjective or adverb)
orthoclay
orthophosphate
Otto fuel (not auto)
outbuildings
outcrop (noun/verb)
outfall

output
outsource
overburden
overflow
overlap
overlie, overlay, overlain
overrun
overwinter

P

packer test, packer-tested
panelboard
parametric
parkland
part-time (adjective)
pass through (verb)
pass-through (noun)
pastureland
pebble-sized
penetrameter
per person (adjective: per person data)
per se (no hyphen or italic)
percent
percent (usually no % except in figures/tables; however, this can vary per company style)
permeability, permeable
persistent
petroleum hydrocarbon-contaminated soils
pH
phase in (verb)
phase out (verb)
phase-in (adjective)
phase-out (adjective)
phenol
photoionization
phreactic
physiography

piezometer, piezometric
pillow block
pilot-scale
pipe lay (if an adjective before a
noun, use pipe-lay)
pipe mill
pipe rack
pipe wall
pipefitting
pipeline
pipework
pitot tube
plan holder
plasterboard
playground
Pleistocene
pole yard
policyholder
policymaker
policy-making
polyethylene
polyurethane
pore water
portland cement
postaccident (adjective:
postaccident data)
post-closure
post-evalution
postmortem (adjective /noun)
posttreatment (adjective)
pot room
pothole
potliner
power line
power pack
power plant
powerhouse
powerstation
practice

pre (generally no hyphen with
pre; see Webster's to be sure)
precede
precursor
predominant (adjective)
predominate (verb)
preestablished
preevaluation
preexisting
preplanned
pressure meter
pretreatment
preventive (not preventative)
principal-in-charge
print out (verb)
printout (noun; adjective)
problem solving (noun)
process area
process water
procure/procured/procuring
project-specific (adjective)
promontory
proof-roll
propellant
pseudoclassical
pull box
pullout
pump house
pump out (verb)
pump station
pump-out (adjective before
noun)
punch list
purge-and-trap method
push-button

Q
quack grass
quantitation
quartzose (adjective)

quasi-permanent

R

radii (plural of radius)
radioactive
rail yard
railcar
railroad
railroad tracks
rain gear
rainfall
rainwater
rangeland
-rate (constant-rate test)
rate setting (noun)
ratemaking
ratepayer
read out (verb)
readout (noun)
real-time
real-time kinematic
reconnaissance
record keeping (noun)
record-keeping (adjective)
re-create (verb; to create again)
-reducing (cost-reducing measures)
reed canary grass
reequilibrated
reestablish
reevaluate
reexamine
regarding or in regard to (not in regards to)
-regulating (temperature-regulating valves)
reinstall
-related (hazardous-waste-related tasks)
remediation

reprint
reproducibility, reproducible
-resistant (corrosion-resistant metal)
resistivity
restroom
re-treat (to treat again)
re-use (adjective, as in re-use planning)
reuse (verb)
right-of-way
rinsate (not rinseate)
rinse water
riprap
riverbank
riverbed
road map
roadbed
roadway
rock fill
rockfall
roll off (verb)
roll up (verb)
-rolled (hot-rolled steel)
roll-off (adjective: roll-off box)
roll-up (adjective: roll-up shades)
-roof (flat-roof building)
rooftop (adjective: rooftop repairs)
rule making (noun)
rule-making (adjective)
rule set
run off (verb)
run on (verb)
run out (verb); run-out (noun)
runoff (noun/adjective)
run-on (adjective /noun)
run-out (noun); run out (verb)

S

salt water (noun)
saltwater (adjective)
sandbag
sandbank
sandblasting, grit
sandpack
sandpaper
-scale (large-scale operations)
scale up (verb)
scaleup (adjective /noun)
scrap yard
seawater
sedimentary
selenium
self-contained
self-feeder
self-monitoring (adjective)
semiannual
semiarid
semiconfined
semilog, semilogarithmic
semivolatile
set aside (verb)
set point
set up (verb)
set-aside (noun)
-setting, (rate-setting goals)
setup (noun)
sewer flow
sewer shed
sewerline
sheepsfoot
sheet iron
sheet metal
sheet metalwork
sheet piles
sheet steel
sheet tin

Sheetrock®
shell-like (but grasslike; check Webster's to be sure)
shipyard
shop blast
shoreline
short range (noun)
short term (adverb/noun)
short-range (adjective)
short-term (adjective)
shut down (verb)
shut off (verb)
shutdown (noun)
shutdown valve
shut-in
shutoff (adjective)
side boom
side slope
side water
side-scan sonar
siliceous
siltstone
single-family residence
single-phase (adjective)
site work
site-specific (adjective: site-specific issue)
sitewide
sledgehammer
-slope (down-slope length)
slug catcher (some companies prefer one word)
smooth sheet
smoothed-in (adjective: smoothed-in roadbed)
snakebite
snowmelt
soil gas (soil gas field survey)
soil-pore liquid

solenoid
solenoid valve
solid waste
sonar
sonication
-source (near-source well)
southernmost
southwest-northeast
southwest-trending
spark-proof
spectrometry,
spectrophotometry
split case
split-spoon sampler
-spoon (split-spoon sample)
spray head
spreadsheet
spring line
stainless steel (noun)
stainless-steel (adjective)
stand-alone (adjective stand-alone document)
standby
stand-off
standpipe
start up (verb)
start-up (adjective/noun)
state of the art (noun)
state-certified
state-of-the-art (adjective)
statewide
static GPS
-status (special-status species)
steady state (noun/adjective)
steam clean (verb)
steam generator
steel making (noun)
steel-making (adjective)
-stem (hollow-stem auger)

step-discharge test
step-down, step-up (noun/adjective)
step-drawdown test
stepwise
stop nut
storativity
storm water (noun)
straightforward
stratigraphy, stratigraphic
stream water
streambank
streambed
streamflow
strength (full-strength test)
stubout (adjective/noun)
sub (generally no hyphen; check Webster's to be sure)
subaerial
subarea
subbasin
subbottom
subcontractor
subsea
subsection
subsurface
subsystem
sulfate, sulfite, sulfitic
sulfur
sulfur, sulfuric, sulfurous
Super Sacks
Superfund
supernate
supersede (not supercede)
surface water
surficial
switch ties
switchgrass
switchyard

syncline, synclinal

T

tailwater

take off (verb)

takeoff (noun/adjective)

talus

tamper-proof

tamper-resistant

tank farm

tannin

tare

task force

task order

teamwork (noun)

tectonic

Teflon® (trademark)

telltale (a type of valve)

test pit

-tested (tightness-tested seal)

through bolt

time frame

time line

time sheet

time-consuming

timeframe

timetable

toolshed

top-of-casing (adjective)

topsoil

total Kjeldahl nitrogen

touch-up

toward (not towards)

-track (fast-track schedule)

trade name

trademark

tradeoff

trans-Alaska oil pipeline (AP style)

Trans-Alaska Pipeline System

(TAPS) (Alyeska style)

transfer/transferring/transferred/transferable/transferal

transmissivity

travel, traveled, traveling

-treated (heat-treated metals)

tremie (adjective, not verb)

trench side

troubleshooting

trunk line

trunnion

truss-joist

t-test

tubesheet

tuffaceous

turbid

turbidity

turbulent (not turbulant)

turnaround

turnaround time

turndown

twofold

two-phased (adjective)

Tyrek®

U

U.S. (not US, and never define U.S.)

U.S.C. (for U.S. Code)

ullage

ultra-high (adjective: ultra-high frequency)

ultraviolet

unconfined

unconformable, unconformity

unconsolidated

under floor (adverb: the mouse was under the floor)

under ground (adverb: the pipe was under the ground)

under water (adverb: the site was under water)
under way (adverb)
undercut
underdeposit
underdraln
underfloor (adjective: underfloor pipe)
underflow
underground (adjective: underground pipe)
underlie, underlay, underlain
underlying
underrun
under-voltage
underwater (adjective: underwater activity)
underway (adjective) (occurring, performed, or used while traveling or in motion: underway replenishment of fuel)
United States (noun), U.S. (adjective)
unsaturated
unthreaded
upbed
updip
upflow
upgradient (adjective: upgradient well)
uphill
uplands
uppermost
uptake
upwind
usable (not useable)
EPA-approved
user friendly

V

vadose zone
Vendor
venturi
Visqueen® (not Visquine)
volatile
volumetric

W

walk through (verb)
walk-through (noun)
-wall (double-wall construction)
wallboard
wash wastes
wash water
washout
waste line
waste load
waste stream
wastewater
water body
water main
water spray
water stop
water table
water well
water-bearing (adjective)
water-bearing unit (modifier)
water-cooled (adjective)
watercourse
waterflood
waterfowl
waterline
waterpower
watershed
watertight
waterwash
waterway
Web site
weekday
weep holes

weldability
weld pack
-well (near-well transmissivity)
well bay
well house
well line
well pad
well point
well screen
well work
wellbore
wellfield
wellhead
well-known (adjective before noun)
well known (after noun)
wellpoint
wellsite
west side
westernmost (but west side)
wet well
wheatgrass
wholly owned
wind up (verb)
windblown
windbreak
windrow (row of heaped matter)
windup (adjective/noun)
wingwall
wireway
wood waste
wood yard
work area
work over (transitive verb; to work over something)
work plan
work scope
work sheet
work site

workday
workers' compensation
workflow
workforce
workload
workman
workover (adjective, as in a hydraulic workover rig)
workplace
workshop
workstation
workweek
worldwide
worst-case scenario
w-test

Y

yard—see backyard, front yard, pole yard, rail yard, shipyard, scrap yard, switchyard, and wood yard
yearlong (adjective)
year-round (adjective)

Z

-zone (trench-zone data

10.0 COMMONLY MISSPELLED WORDS

absence
abundance
accessible
accidentally
acclaim
accommodate
accomplish
accordion
accumulate
achievement
acquaintance
across
address
advertisement
aggravate
alleged
annual
apparent
appearance
argument
atheist
athletics
attendance
auxiliary
balloon
barbecue
barbiturate
bargain
basically
beggar
beginning
believe
biscuit

bouillon
boundary
Britain
business
calendar
camouflage
cantaloupe
category
cemetery
chagrined
challenge
characteristic
changing
chief
cigarette
climbed
collectible
colonel
colossal
column
coming
committee
commitment
comparative
competent
completely
concede
conceive
condemn
conscientious
consciousness
consistent
continuous

controlled
coolly
corollary
convenient
correlate
correspondence
counselor
courteous
courtesy
criticize
deceive
defendant
deferred
dependent
descend
description
desirable
despair
desperate
develop
development
difference
dilemma
dining
disappearance
disappoint
disastrous
discipline
disease
dispensable
dissatisfied
dominant
drunkenness
easily
ecstasy
efficiency
eighth
either
eligible

emperor
enemy
entirely
equipped
equivalent
escape
especially
exaggerate
exceed
excellence
excellent
exhaust
existence
expense
experience
experiment
explanation
extremely
exuberance
fallacious
fallacy
familiar
fascinate
feasible
February
fictitious
finally
financially
forcibly
foreign
forfeit
formerly
foresee
forty
fourth
fulfill
fundamentally
gauge
generally

genius	intercede
government	interference
governor	interpret
grievous	interrupt
guarantee	introduce
guerrilla	irrelevant
guidance	irresistible
handkerchief	island
happily	jealousy
harass	jewelry
height	judicial
heinous	knowledge
hemorrhage	laboratory
heroes	legitimate
hesitancy	leisure
hindrance	length
hoarse	lenient
hoping	license
humorous	lieutenant
hypocrisy	lightning
hypocrite	likelihood
ideally	likely
idiosyncrasy	loneliness
ignorance	losing
imaginary	lovely
immediately	luxury
implement	magazine
incidentally	maintain
incredible	maintenance
independence	manageable
independent	maneuver
indicted	marriage
indispensable	mathematics
inevitable	medicine
influential	millennium
information	millionaire
inoculate	miniature
insurance	minutes
intelligence	mischievous

missile	parallel
misspelled	parliament
mortgage	particularly
mosquito	pavilion
mosquitoes	peaceable
murmur	peculiar
muscle	penetrate
mysterious	perceive
narrative	performance
naturally	permanent
necessary	permissible
necessity	permitted
neighbor	perseverance
neutron	persistence
ninety	physical
ninth	physician
noticeable	picnicking
nowadays	piece
nuisance	pilgrimage
obedience	pitiful
obstacle	planning
occasion	pleasant
occasionally	portray
occurred	possess
occurrence	possessive
official	potato
omission	potatoes
omit	practically
omitted	prairie
opinion	preference
opponent	preferred
opportunity	prejudice
oppression	preparation
optimism	prescription
ordinarily	prevalent
origin	primitive
outrageous	privilege
overrun	probably
panicky	procedure

proceed	sacrifice
professor	safety
prominent	salary
pronounce	satellite
pronunciation	scenery
propaganda	schedule
psychology	secede
publicly	secretary
pursue	seize
quandary	separate
quarantine	sergeant
questionnaire	several
quizzes	shepherd
realistically	shining
realize	similar
really	simile
recede	simply
receipt	sincerely
receive	skeptic
recognize	skeptical
recommend	skiing
reference	soliloquy
referred	sophomore
relevant	souvenir
relieving	specifically
religious	specimen
remembrance	sponsor
reminiscence	spontaneous
repetition	statistics
representative	stopped
resemblance	strategy
reservoir	strength
resistance	strenuous
restaurant	stubbornness
rheumatism	subordinate
rhythm	subtle
rhythmical	succeed
roommate	success
sacrilegious	succession

sufficient	transferred
supersede	truly
suppress	twelfth
surprise	tyranny
surround	unanimous
susceptible	undoubtedly
suspicious	unnecessary
syllable	until
symmetrical	usage
synonymous	usually
tangible	vacuum
technical	valuable
technique	vengeance
temperature	vigilant
tendency	village
themselves	villain
theories	violence
therefore	visible
thorough	warrant
though	Wednesday
through	weird
till	wherever
tomorrow	wholly
tournament	yacht
tourniquet	yield
tragedy	zoology

11.0 COMMONLY CONFUSED WORDS

Any handbook such as those used in college English courses should suffice to answer most English usage questions. Still, the most common errors are included here for your reference and for clarification. (Sources include *The St. Martin's Handbook* and *The Simon & Schuster Handbook for Writers*, as well as from my own experience editing and teaching.)

a, an. Use "a" with a word that begins with a consonant (a forest), with a sounded h (a hemisphere, a history), or with another consonant sound such as "you" or "wh" (a euphoric moment, a one-sided match, a 1,000-gallon tank). Use "an" with a word that begins with a vowel (an umbrella), with a silent h (an honor), or with a vowel sound (an X-ray). (I often see writers get confused by the "h" rule and write "an history," for example; the test is if it's a sounded h, use "a" not "an.")

accept, except. The verb accept means "receive" or "agree to." *Melanie will accept the job offer.* The preposition except means "aside from" or "excluding." *All the plaintiffs except Mr. Smith decided to accept the settlement offered by the defendant.*

absorption, adsorption. Absorption means to soak up, like a sponge; dissolving in liquid or gas. Adsorption refers to when one entity adheres to another, as in carbon adsorption, where a molecule adheres to the activated carbon surface.

advice, advise. Advice is a noun meaning opinion or suggestion; advise is a verb meaning offer or provide advice. *Jenna advised Sally that Frank's advice was poor.*

affect, effect. Affect is a verb meaning influence or move the emotions of. Effect is a noun meaning result, or, less commonly, a verb meaning bring about. Use the "the" test. If you can put "the" in front of it, you have a noun and effect. *The effect of the rain was a flood.* If "the" can only go after the word, use affect, as in: *The rain affected the roof by causing it to break.*

all ready, already. All ready means fully prepared. Already means previously. We were all ready for Lucy's party when we learned that she had already left.

all right. Always write "all right" as two words.

a lot. A lot is always two words. Avoid in formal (i.e., technical) writing.

a.m., p.m. Use only with numbers, not as substitutes for the words morning, afternoon, or evening.

among, between. Use between for two items or people and among for three or more items or people. *The relationship between the twins is different front that among the other three children.*

amount, number. Use amount for quantities that you cannot count (singular nouns such as water, light, or power). Use number for quantities that you can count (usually plural nouns such as objects or people). *A small number of volunteers cleared a large amount of brush within a few hours.*

and/or. Avoid if possible. Use x, y, or both instead.(I generally try to avoid the slash because it is confusing and seems like lazy writing.)

anion, cation. Anion is an ion with a negative charge; cation is an ion with a positive charge.

any body, anybody, any one, anyone. Note the differences: *Although anyone could enjoy carving wood, not just anybody could make a sculpture like that. Any body of water has its own distinctive ecology. Customers were allowed to buy only two sale items at any one time.*

anyway, anyways. Use anyway, never anyways.

as, because. Avoid using "as" for "because" or when in sentences where its meaning is not clear. For example, does *Carl left town as his father was arriving* mean at the same time as his father was arriving or because his father was arriving?

as, like, such as. For comparisons, use "as" when comparing two qualities that people or objects possess. *The box is as wide as it is long.* Also use "as" to identify equivalent terms in a description. *Gary served as moderator at the town meeting.* Use "like" to indicate similarity but not equivalency: *Hugo, like Jane, was a detailed observer.* In formal writing, "such as" is preferable to "like" in most cases.

assure, ensure, insure. Assure means convince or promise, and its direct object is usually a person or persons. *The candidate assured the voters he would not raise taxes.* Ensure and insure both mean make certain, but insure is usually used in the specialized sense of protection against financial loss. *When the city began water rationing to ensure that the supply would last, the Browns found that they could no longer afford to insure their car wash business.* (Note that some companies avoid using "ensure" as it promises too much: *We will ensure that the site is cleaned up by May 15, 2015.*)

as to. Do not use as to as a substitute for about. *Connie was unsure about* (not as to) *David's intentions.*

because of, due to. Both phrases are used to describe the relationship between a cause and an effect. Use due to when the effect (a noun) is stated first and followed by the verb to be. *His illness was due to malnutrition.* (Illness, a noun, is the effect.) Use because of, not due to, when the effect is a clause, not a noun. *He was sick because of malnutrition.* (He was sick, a clause, is the effect.)

being as, being that. Avoid these expressions (substitutes for because) in formal writing.

beside, besides. Beside, a preposition, means next to. Besides is either a preposition meaning other than or in addition to or an adverb meaning moreover. *No one besides Elaine knows whether the tree is still growing beside the house.*

bi, semi. Bi means every other, and semi means twice in a given period.

breath, breathe. Breath is the noun, and breathe is the verb.

but, yet, however. Use these words separately, not together.

but that, but what. Avoid these as substitutes for that.

can, may. Can refers to ability and may to possibility or permission to do something. *Since I can ski the slalom well, I may win the race. May I leave early to practice?*

can't, couldn't. Avoid all contractions in formal writing.

choose, chose. Choose is the simple form of the verb; chose is the past-tense form. *I chose the movie last week, so you choose it tonight.*

compare to, compare with. Compare to means describe one thing as similar to another. *Juanita compared the noise to the roar of a waterfall.* Compare with is the more general activity of noting similarities and differences between objects or people. *The detective compared the latest photograph with the old one, noting how the man's appearance had changed.*

complement, compliment. Complement means go well with or enhance. Compliment means praise.

comprise, compose. Comprise means contain (the whole comprises the parts). Compose means make up (the parts compose the whole). *The class comprises 20 students. Twenty students compose the class.*

consequently, subsequently. Consequently means as a result or therefore. Subsequently just means afterwards. Roger lost his job, and subsequently I lost mine. Consequently, I was unable to pay my rent.

continual, continuous. Continual describes an activity that is repeated at regular or frequent intervals. Continuous describes either an activity that is ongoing without interruption or an object that is connected without break. *The damage done by continuous erosion was increased by the continual storms.*

couple of. Avoid in formal writing. Say specifically what you mean.

criteria, criterion. Criterion means a standard of judgment or a necessary qualification. Criteria is the plural form.

data. The word data is the plural form of the Latin word datum, meaning a fact or a result collected during research. Treat data as plural in formal writing. *These data indicate that fewer people smoke today than 10 years ago.*

different from, different than. Different from is generally preferred in formal writing.

discreet, discrete. Discreet means tactful or prudent. Discrete means distinct or separate. *The dean's discreet encouragement brought representatives of all the discrete factions to the meeting.*

dispose, dispose of. Dispose means to incline or to be inclined toward something. Dispose of means to throw away.

disinterested, uninterested. Disinterested means unbiased or impartial. Uninterested means not interested or indifferent.

elicit, illicit. The verb elicit means to draw out or evoke. The adjective illicit means illegal.

especially, specially. Especially means very or particularly. Specially means for a special reason or purpose. *The audience especially enjoyed the new composition, specially written for the holiday.*

every day, everyday. Everyday is an adjective used to describe something as ordinary or common. Every day is an adjective modifying a noun, specifying which particular day. I ride the subway every day even though pushing and shoving are everyday occurrences.

every one, everyone. Everyone is an indefinite pronoun; every one is a noun modified by an adjective, referring to each member of a group. Because he began the assignment after everyone else, David knew that he could finish every one of the selections.

explicit, implicit. Explicit means directly or openly expressed. Implicit means indirectly expressed or implied. *The explicit message of the advertisement urged consumers to buy the product while the implicit message promised popularity.*

farther, further. Farther refers to physical distance. *How much farther is it to the jobsite?* Further refers to time or degree. *I want to avoid further delays and further misunderstandings.*

fewer, less. Use fewer with objects or people that can be counted (plural nouns). Use less with amounts that cannot be counted (singular nouns). *The world would be safer with fewer bombs and less* *hostility.*

firstly, secondly, thirdly. These are old-fashioned for introducing a series of points. Use first, second, and third.

following. Following is an adjective (the following items) or a noun (a large following), not a substitute for after. *After the holes were dug*, not *Following the hole digging.*

from . . . to, between . . . and. These have different meanings. *The store operated from 1950 to 1970.* This means the store was open from the year 1950 to the year 1970. *The store operated between 1950 and 1970.* This means the store was open from 1951 to 1969. *Concentrations were detected from 5 mg/kg to 10 mg/kg.* The concentrations, in this case, were from 5 mg/kg to 10 mg/kg. *Concentrations detected were between 5 mg/kg and 100 mg/kg.* In this case, the concentrations were from 6 (or 5.1 . . . anything higher than 5) mg/kg to 99 (or 99.9 . . . anything lower than 100) mg/kg.

good, well. Good is an adjective and should not be used as a substitute for the adverb well. Gabriel is a good host who cooks quite well.

has got to, has to. Avoid these colloquial phrases for must.

have, of. *Have*, not *of*, should follow could, would, should, or might.

he/she, his/her. He/she and his/her are ungainly ways to avoid sexism in writing. Other solutions are to write out *he or she* or to alternate using *he* and *she*. But perhaps the best solution is the eliminate the pronouns entirely or to make the subject plural (they), thereby avoiding all reference to gender. *Everyone should carry his or her driver's license with him or her* could be revised to *Drivers should carry driver's licenses at all times* or to *People should carry their driver's licenses with them.*

hopefully. Hopefully is widely misused to mean it is hoped, but its correct meaning is with hope. Sam watched the roulette wheel hopefully, not Hopefully, Sam will win.

if, whether. Use whether or whether or not (I prefer to just use "whether" without the "or not") to express an alternative. *She was considering whether to buy the new software.* Reserve if for the subjunctive case. *If it should rain tomorrow, our class will meet in the gym.*

impact. As a noun, impact means a forceful collision. As a verb, impact means pack together. *Because they were impacted, Jason's wisdom teeth needed to be removed.* Avoid the colloquial use of impact as a vague word meaning to affect. *Population control may reduce* (not impact) *world hunger.* (Note: I see "impact" used frequently by my clients when "affected" would probably be a better choice such as "the area will not be impacted by construction"; since it is so commonly used and seems to have become acceptable for such use, I often leave as is. Here is a typical example: *To determine the extent of petroleum-hydrocarbon impacted soils in the areas of confirmed impact. . .*
.

imply, infer. To imply is to suggest. To infer is to make an educated guess. Speakers and writers imply; listeners and readers infer. *Beth and Peter's letter implied that they were planning a very small wedding; we inferred that we would not be invited.*

inside, inside of, outside, outside of. Drop of after the prepositions inside and outside. The class regularly met outside the building.

interact with, interface with. Avoid these colloquial expressions.

irregardless, regardless. Regardless is the correct word; irregardless is a double negative.

is when, is where. These vague and faulty shortcuts should be avoided in definitions. *Schizophrenia is a psychotic condition in which* (not when or where) *a person withdraws from reality.*

its, it's. Its is a possessive pronoun, even though it does not have an apostrophe. It's is a contraction for it is; avoid it's and other contractions in formal writing.

lay, lie. Lay means place or put. Its forms are lay, laid, laying, laid, and laid. It generally has a direct object, specifying what has been placed. *She laid her books on the desk.* Lie means recline or be positioned and does not take a direct object. Its forms are lie, lay, lain, lying. *She lay awake until 2 a.m., worrying about the exam.* Funny (and true) story: I was showing a friend of mine how well trained my dog was. I said, "Lay down," and she did not move. My friend said, "Well of course she's not moving; you are using incorrect grammar. You should have said lie down!" He was right, of course. Another incorrect example: In the song "Lay Lady Lay," the phrase "Lay across my big brass bed," should actually be "Lie across my big brass bed."

like, such as. Both like and such as may be used in a statement giving an example or a series of examples. Like means similar to; use "like" when comparing the subject mentioned to the examples. *A hurricane, like a flood or any other major disaster, may strain a region's emergency resources.* Use "such as" when the examples represent a general category of things or people. "Such as" is often used as an alternative to for example. *A destructive hurricane, such as Gilbert in 1988, may drastically alter an area's economy.* Commas are not always necessary before and after the phrase containing such as. *Adding fruits such as apples and pears to the bowl should enhance its appearance.* In technical writing, I often use "e.g." instead of such as or for example: *The majority of residents also depend upon fish and game (e.g., trout, salmon, bear, and moose) obtained through subsistence hunting and fishing activities.*

loose, lose. Lose is a verb meaning misplace. Loose, as an adjective, means not securely attached. *Tighten that loose screw before you lose it.*

lots, lots of. Avoid in formal writing.

may be, maybe. May be is a verb phrase. Maybe, the adverb, means perhaps. *She may be the president today, but maybe she will lose the next election.*

media. Media, the plural form of medium, takes a plural verb. The media are going to cover the council meeting.

Ms. Use Ms. instead of Miss or Mrs. unless a woman specifies another title before her name. Ms. should appear before her first name, not before her husband's name: *Ms. Jane Tate*, not Ms. John Tate.

nor, or. Use "either" with "or" and "neither" with "nor."

off of. Use off rather than off of. The spaghetti slipped off the plate.

on, upon. Upon is old-fashioned; usually, "on" is all you need.

only. When you see the word "only" in a sentence, make sure it is in the correct place. The misplacement of the word "only" can completely change a sentence's meaning. *Emily sang only four songs.* (She could have sang many more, but she did not.) *Emily only sang four songs.* (Did Emily just sing a cappella and not play the songs as well? This is confusing.) *Only Emily sang for the guests.* (Perhaps there were numerous other singers, but they did not sing?) *Emily sang four songs only for the invited guests.* (So staff and uninvited guests could not hear her?)

ordnance, ordinance. Ordnance refers to military supplies such as weapons, ammunition, and combat vehicles. Ordinance refers to a decree or order.

owing to the fact that. Avoid this and other unnecessarily word expressions for because.

percent, percentage. These words identify a number as a fraction of 100. Because they show exact statistics, these terms should not be used casually to mean portion, amount, or number. Generally, the word "percent" is always used with a number while "percentage" is not. *Last year, 70 percent of the dogs at animal control were adopted.* In formal writing, spell out percent rather than using its symbol (%) (However, I often use the % symbol in tables.) Percentage is not used with a specific number. *A large percentage of the population prefers fruit to vegetables.*

precede, proceed. Both are verbs; precede means "come before," and proceed means continue or go forward. *Despite the storm that preceded the campus flooding, we proceeded to class.*

principal, principle. These words are unrelated but are often confused because of their similar spellings. Principal as a noun, refers to a head official or an amount of money loaned or invested. When used as an adjective, principal means most significant. The word meaning a fundamental law, belief, or standard is principle. When Albert was sent to the principal, he defended himself with the principle of free speech. The principal intent of the document was to inform.

raise, rise. Raise means lift or move upward. In the case of children, it means bring up or rear. As a transitive verb, it takes a direct object—someone raises something. *The wedding guests raised their glasses in celebration.* Rise means go upwards. It is not followed by a direct object; something rises by itself. *She saw the steam rise from the kettle and knew the tea was ready.*

respectfully, respectively. Respectfully means with respect. Respectively means in the order given. The brothers, respectively a juggler and an acrobat, respectfully greeted the audience.

set, sit. Set means put or place, and it is followed by a direct object—the thing that is placed. Sit does not take a direct object and refers to the action of taking a seat. *Amelia sat at the picnic table and set her backpack on the ground.*

since. Since has two meanings. The first meaning shows the passage of time (*I have not eaten since Tuesday*); the second and more informal meaning is because (*Since you are in a bad mood, I will go away*). Be careful not to write sentences in which since is ambiguous in meaning. *Since I had knee surgery, I have been doing nothing but watching television.* (Since here could mean either because or ever since. In order to avoid such problems some writers prefer not to use since to mean because.)

some body, somebody, some one, someone. *When somebody comes walking down the hall, I always hope that it is someone I know. In dealing with some body like the senate, arrange to meet consistently some one person who can represent the group.*

stationary, stationery. Stationary is an adjective meaning standing still. Stationery is a noun meaning writing paper or materials. *When the bus was stationary at the train crossing, Karen took out her stationery and wrote a letter.*

than, then. Use the conjunction "than" in comparative statements. *The truck was bigger than my house.* Use the adverb "then" when referring to a sequence of events or emotions. *Jim finished college, and then he went to graduate school.*

that, which. That, always followed by a restrictive clause, singles out the object being described. *The trip that you took to New York was expensive.* Note that the clause after "that" is essential to the meaning; it cannot be deleted. Which may be followed by either a restrictive or a nonrestrictive clause but often is used only with the latter. The which clause may simply add more information about a noun or noun clause, and it is set off by commas. *My house, which is in Palmer, is a two-story duplex.* You can delete the phrase in between the commas and still keep the main idea of the sentence that you want to get across. But you cannot delete the words following *that* without losing the meaning of the sentence. *The book that is on the table is the one I want.*

their, there, they're. "Their" is a pronoun, the possessive form of they. *The clients showed their drawings to the editor.* "There" refers to a place. *There, dinosaurs used to walk.* There also is used with the verb "be" in expletive constructions (there is, there are). *There are three items on the agenda.* (I usually try to edit out "there is" and "there are" as they are unnecessary phrases: *The three items on the agenda are dogs, cats, and elephants.*) They're is a contraction of they are, and, like all contractions, it should be avoided in formal writing.

to, too, two. To is a preposition, generally showing direction or nearness. *Stan drove to Eugene.* Avoid using to after where. *Where are you driving?* (not driving to) Too means also. *I am driving there too.* Two is the number.

toward, towards. Towards is considered archaic; toward is now preferred (per Webster's).

visible, visual. Visible means capable of being seen, while visual means pertaining to sight. *No holes were visible in the tank. The method of examination was visual.*

where. Use where alone, not with prepositions such as at or to. *Where did he drill?* (not drill at)

which, who, that. When referring to ideas or things, use which or that. When referring to people, use who or whom. *My aunt, who was furious, pushed on the door, which was still stuck. The book that I like best is Old Yeller. The teacher whom I like best is Ms. Pastorelli. People who are interested can sign up after class.*

Interestingly, animals can be referred to by either who or that, depending on the writer's view of them. Sometimes people refer to pets by using the word who and wild animals by using the word that. *Woody, who is my best friend, is a collie. The wolf that ate the rabbits is now in a pen.*

who, whom. Use who if the following clause begins with a verb. *Monica, who drinks uncontrollably, is my godmother. Monica, who is my godmother, drinks uncontrollably.* Use whom in the following clause, which begins with a pronoun. *I have heard that Monica, whom I have not seen for 10 years, wears only purple.* An exception occurs when a verbal phrase such as *I think* comes between who and the following clause. Ignore such a phrase as you decide which form to use. *Monica, who (I think) wears nothing but purple, is my godmother.* Here is a simple way to remember this rule: Can you replace the word with "she"? If so, use who. Can you replace the word with "her" or "them"? If so, use whom. (The phrase "whom I have not seen" becomes "I have not seen her" as you apply this test.)

who's, whose. Who's is the contraction of who and is. Avoid contractions in formal writing. Whose is possessive. *Whose book is on the counter?*

your, you're. Your shows possession. *Bring your pets to the party.* You're is the contraction of you and are. Avoid contractions in formal writing.

12.0   TERMS AND DEFINITIONS

It is a good idea to create a list of commonly used terms and definitions for your company, so that your list can be added to and pulled from for future documents. It is especially important to have a consistent understanding and definition of a term for all personnel.

The following definitions are from q wonderful free online source titled *Definitions of Civil Engineering Terms* by Talal Ahmed Kamal, which is available as a free PDF at various Web sites (including crazyengineers.com). There are also various Web sites (such as engineering-dictionary.org) and reference books that provide definitions. I have just selected a few to provide you with an example list.

For your own company, select various documents and begin keeping a separate one with the terms defined. Keep them in alphabetical order. You might submit the document of terms to various authors in your company to check them over and make sure they agree that each definition is the one your company will use. This document will be updated as needed.

Abutment
A concrete support wall constructed at both ends of a bridge or an arch, in order to resist the horizontal force from the bridge or the arch, support the ends of the bridge span and to prevent the bank from sliding under.

Accelerator
A substance such as calcium chloride ($CaCl2$), added in small quantities (max. 0.03% of the cement) to plain concrete to hasten its hardening rate, its set or both.

Acquisition
The process of obtaining Right-of-Way.

Active Earth Pressure
The horizontal push from earth onto a wall. The active earth force from sand on to a free retaining wall is equivalent to that from a fluid of density 0.25 to 0.30 times that of the sand. The force from sand on to a fixed retaining wall is very much more.

Addendum or Addenda
Written instruments or documents issued prior to the execution of a contract to modify or revise the bidding documents.

Adhesion or Bond
The sticking together of structural parts by mechanical or chemical bonding using a cement or glue.

Admixture or Additive
A substance other than aggregate, cement or water, added in small quantities to the concrete mix to alter its properties or those of the hard concrete. The most important admixtures for concrete are accelerators, air-entraining agents, plasticizers and retarders.

Affidavit of Non-Collusion
A sworn statement, by bidders for the same work, that their proposal prices were arrived at independently without consultation or a secret agreement or cooperation for a fraudulent or deceitful purpose between or among them.

Agent
The person who legally represents the contractor and acts for him on all occasions. He is often a Civil Engineer.

Air-Entrained Concrete
A concrete used for constructing roads. It has about 5% air and is therefore less dense than ordinary good concrete, but it has excellent freeze-thaw resistance. The strength loss is roughly 5% for each 1% air entrained. Air entrained concrete produced by adding an admixture to concrete or cement, which drags small bubbles of air (Smaller than 1 mm in diameter) into the concrete mix. The bubbles increase the workability and allowing both sand and water contents to be reduced.

Alignment
(1) The fixing of points on the ground in the correct lines for setting out a road, railway, wall, transmission line, canal, etc. (2) A ground plan showing a route, as opposed to a profile or section, which shows levels and elevations.

13.0 ACRONYMS AND ABBREVIATIONS MOST COMMONLY USED AT OUR COMPANY

13.1 Overview

Since this is the first version of our company's style guide, this list of acronyms and abbreviations is a work in progress. Please let the technical editor know of any missing acronyms/abbreviations or of any mistakes in this list. In the meantime, here are some of the acronyms that are currently used in our company's documents, as well as some that might be used in future documents. Again, the most important thing to remember is to be consistent within documents and within the company. Therefore, use this list as a guide for capitalization rules, spelling, and definitions of acronyms. For example, use ArcInfo as presented here instead of ARC/INFO or Arc/Info. *Although all of these forms of ArcInfo have been used in XYZ Company's documents, we have chosen one (based on ESRI's Web site) to use in our documents from now on.*

Note: These are acronyms and abbreviations taken from various company lists and government agency Web site lists; some may not be relevant to your firm, some names may have changed, and your style may be different for others. We suggest that you make notes on your hard copy of which ones to delete, change, or add, as you (or your technical editors) use this document.

If you have purchased our Microsoft Word version of this style guide at our Web site (www.wordsworthwriting.net or www.formsinword.com), you can paste in your own acronym list. We suggest that you paste special, and then select unformatted text, anywhere in the acronym list. Then you can select all the acronyms (the ones here and the new list you have inserted) and choose Table and Sort by paragraph, and you will automatically alphabetize everything. This should save you a lot of time!

Please do let us know (e-mail editor@wordsworthwriting.net) if you see anything that should be changed.

13.2   General Guidelines

General rules for using acronyms and abbreviations follow:

- Always spell out a word or term when it is first used in the text, followed by the acronym or abbreviation in parentheses. You can use the acronym from then on. Examples: The U.S. Environmental Protection Agency (USEPA) and the Alaska Department of Fish and Game (ADF&G) agree that . . .

- It is not necessary to use acronyms. For items appearing only once or twice in a text, it is better to spell them out.

- Standard company style is to include an acronym list at the beginning of each report or proposal. This does not preclude defining each acronym first use, however.

- Please add, delete, and change as you see fit, and turn in your suggestions to the technical editor.

- Certain acronyms and abbreviations are included here that will only be used in figures and tables if needed for spacing, never in the text. Examples include SYST for system.

- Some companies and agencies capitalize all words in their acronyms list, but I do not. I follow the correct capitalization for that term.

13.3   Acronyms & Abbreviations

%	use for "percent" only in table/graph/equation
μCi	microcurie(s)
μg	microgram(s)
μg/kg	microgram(s) per kilogram
μg/L	microgram(s) per liter
μm	micrometer(s) (avoid outdated "micron" per U.S. Government Printing Office and NBS Special Publication 330)
'	instead of apostrophe, use minute or foot in text
"	instead of quotation mark, use second or inch in text
°C	degrees Celsius
°F	degrees Fahrenheit
0_3	ozone
18 AAC 80	18 = chapter number, AAC = Alaska Administrative

	Code, 80 = section number
A	ampere; air
A&G	administrative and general
a.m.	ante meridian (before noon) (do not define in text)
A/E	architect/engineer, architectural/engineering
A/E/C	architect/engineer/construction (or architectural, engineering, and construction)
A/M	availability/maintainability
A/S	activated sludge
AA	atomic absorption (spectrophotometry)
AAAC	all-aluminum alloy conductor
AAC	Alaska Administrative Code; acceptable ambient concentration
AADT	average annual daily traffic
AAL	acceptable ambient level, applied action level
AAPG	American Association of Petroleum Geologists
AAQS	ambient air quality standard
AASHTO	American Association of State Highway and Transportation Officials
AATDF	Advanced Applied Technology Demonstration Facility
ABC	activity-based charging
ABCC	Atomic Bomb Casualty Commission
ABDN	as-built discrepancy notification
ABDT	auxiliary building drain tank
ABF	activated biological filter
ABIH	American Board of Industrial Hygienists
ABP	as-built package
ABPS	auxiliary building passageway sump
ABS	auxiliary building sump; acrylonitrile-butadiene-styrene
ac	alternating current; acre
AC	asbestos-cement
ACA	ammoniacal copper arsenate
ACAS	Architect-Engineer Contract Administration Support System
ACB	air circuit breaker
ACC	accumulator
ACCA	Air Conditioning Contractors of America
ACDP	air contaminant discharge permit
ACEC	American Consulting Engineers Council
ACEEE	American Council for an Energy Efficient Economy
acfm	actual cubic feet per minute
ac-ft	acre-foot (volume of water 1 foot deep and 1 acre in

	area)
ACGIH	American Conference of Governmental Industrial Hygienists
ACI	American Concrete Institute
ACL	alternative concentration limit; alternative cleanup level, Alternative Concentration Limit (EPA),
ACM	asbestos-containing material
ACO	assistant control operator
ACP	administrative control procedure, Air Carcinogen Policy
ACRS	Advisory Committee on Reactor Safeguards
ACS	American Chemical Society, Alaska Communications System)
ACSL	approved contractors and suppliers list
ACSM	American Congress on Surveying and Mapping
ACTR	actuator
ACWA	Oregon Association of Clean Water Agencies
ACWD	Alameda County Water District (California)
ACZA	arsenic, copper, zinc, and ammonia
AD	analog-to-digital (adjective, *e.g.*, AD converter)
ADA	Americans with Disabilities Act
ADC	analog-to-digital converter
ADCOM	Advisory Committee
ADD	average-day demand
ADDS	average-day dry-sea-son (adjective)
ADDW	average-day dry-weather (adjective)
ADEC	Alaska Department of Environmental Conservation
ADEQ	Arizona Department of Environmental Quality
ADF	average daily flow
ADF&G	Alaska Department of Fish and Game
ADI	acceptable daily intake
ADL	Alaska Department of Labor
ADNR	Alaska Department of Natural Resources
ADP	automated data processing; adenosine diphosphate
ADR	absolute drift indication
ADS	auto dispatch signal
ADSS	air data screening system
ADT	average daily traffic
ADWC	average dry-weather capacity
ADWF	average dry-weather flow
ADWS	average-day wet-season (adjective)
AE	action engineer
A-E	Architect-Engineer

AEC	Atomic Energy Commission (now NRC); alternate emergency coordinator, Army Environmental Center (USAEC now preferred)
AEE	Association of Energy Engineers
AEF	Atomic Industries Forum
AEG	Association of Engineering Geologists
AERM	alternate emergency response manager
AF	audio frequency, air force (see USAF)
AFB	Air Force Base
AFB	auxiliary fuel building; air force base (capitalize if part of full name, as in Elmendorf Air Force Base)
AFCEE	Air Force Center for Environmental Excellence
AFD	axial flux differential
AFDC	allowance for funds used during constriction
AFFF	aqueous film-forming foam
AFI	Air Filter Institute
AFP	auxiliary feedwater pump (use AFWP instead)
AFRC	Air Force Reserve Command
AFRC	assistant field team coordinator, Air Force Reserve Command
AFS	Air Force Station
AFS	auxiliary feedwater system (use AFWS instead)
AFSWC	Air Force Special Weapons Center
AFW	auxiliary feedwater
AFWP	auxiliary feedwater pump
AFWS	auxiliary feedwater system
Ag	silver
AGA	automatic gas analyzer; American Gas Association
AGC	automatic gain control
AGI	Association for Geographic Information
AGI	Applied Geotechnology, Inc., American Geological Institute
AGI	Association for Geographic Information
AGMA	American Gear Manufacturers' Association
AGT	aboveground tank (see AST for aboveground storage tank, preferred)
AGWSE	Association of Ground Water Scientists and Engineers
AHC	available soil water-holding capacity
AHERA	Asbestos Hazard Emergency Response Act of 1986
AHM	acutely hazardous material
AIA	American Insurance Association; American Institute of Architects

AICHE	American Institute of Chemical Engineers
AICP	American Institute of Certified Planners
AIEE	American Institute of Electrical Engineers (now IEEE)
AIME	American Institute of Metallurgical, Mining, and Petroleum Engineers; American Institute of Mining Engineers
AISC	American Institute of Steel Construction
AISI	American Iron and Steel Institute
AK	Alaska
Al	aluminum
AL	analytical limit; Alabama; action level
ALARA	as low as reasonably achievable
ALGOL	algorithmic language
ALP	Airport Layout Plan
ALS	approach lighting system
ALT	ambient laboratory testing; alternative; alternate
ALTM	Airborne Laser Terrain Mapper
AM	amplitude modulation
AML	ARC Macro Language
amp	ampere (shortened word, not abbreviation)
AMSAC	anticipated transient without scram mitigating system actuation circuitry
AMSL	above mean sea level
aMW	average megawatt(s)
AMWA	American Medical Writers Association
ANI	American Nuclear Insurers; American nuclear inspector
ANII	authorized nuclear in-service inspector
ANOVA	analysis of variance
ANS	American Nuclear Society; American Nuclear Standard (document)
ANSI	American National Standards Institute
ANWR	Arctic National Wildlife Refuge
AO	administrative order; auxiliary operator; air Operated (adverb); air-operated (adjective, e.g., AO valve)
AOC	administrative order on consent
AOR	area of review
AOS	assistant operations supervisor
AOV	air-operated valve
AP	audit plan; acceptance plan; administrative procedure; action plan
APC	air pollution control
APCA	Air Pollution Control Association (California)

APCD	Air Pollution Control District (California)
APCO	air pollution control officer (California)
APCS	Air Pollution Control System
APCSB	Auxiliary Power Conversion Systems Branch (of the NRC)
APEG	alkaline metal/polyethylene glycol
APHA	American Public Health Association
API	Application Program Interface; American Petroleum Institute
APM	assistant project manager
APR	air-purifying respirator
APUC	Alaska Public Utilities Commission
APWA	American Public Works Association
AQ	augmented quality
AR	accounts receivable; acknowledgment of receipt; Arkansas
ARAR	applicable or relevant and appropriate requirement
ARCC	active and reactive current compensator
ArcInfo	computer mapping software (an ESRI computer program)
ArcView	(An ESRI computer program)
ARD	automatic ringdown (e.g., ARD phone system)
AREA	American Railway Engineering Association
ARG	annunciator response guide
ARI	all rods in; Air Conditioning and Refrigeration Institute
ARM	area radiation monitor
ARMS	area radiation monitoring system
ARO	all rods out
AROMS	automated remote organic monitoring system
ARPA	Automatic Radar Plotting Aid
ARR	acclimation, release, and recapture
ARRC	Alaska Railroad Corporation
ARS	aerial radio system
As	arsenic
ASA	American Standards Association (now USASI); American Society of Agronomy
ASAP	as soon as possible
ASB	Auxiliary Systems Branch (of the NRC)
ASC	auxiliary safeguards cabinet
ASCE	American Society of Civil Engineers
ASCET	American Society of Certified Engineering Technicians
ASCII	American Standard Code for Information Interchange

ASFO	amended stipulation and final order
ASHRAE	American Society of Heating, Refrigeration, and Air Conditioning Engineers
ASI	auxiliary systems instrumentation; Alternative Services, Inc.
ASIL	acceptable source impact level
ASL	above sea level
ASL	approved suppliers list
ASLAB	Atomic Safety and Licensing Appeal Board
ASLB	Atomic Safety and Licensing Board
ASM	area sensor module
ASME	American Society of Mechanical Engineers
ASPIS	Abandoned Sites Program Information System (database, California)
ASR	aquifer storage and recovery
AST	aboveground storage tank
ASTM	American Society for Testing and Materials
ASWAT	Air Solid Waste Assessment Test
AT	accumulator tank
ATA	air and training admixture
ATD	aerobic thermophilic digestion
ATDC	after top dead center
ATESI	Advanced Technology Engineering Systems, Inc.
atm	atmosphere
ATP	adenosine triphosphate
ATTIC	Alternative Treatment Technology Information Center
ATV	all-terrain vehicle
ATWS	anticipated transient without scram
AUNI	animal unit month(s)
AVB	antivibration bar
AVHRR	Advanced Very High Resolution Radiometer
AVI	Alaska Village Initiatives
AVT	all-volatile treatment
AWARE	avoid waste and reduce emissions
AWB	Association of Washington Businesses
AWG	American wire gauge (e.g., AWG cold lead wires)
AWMA	Air and Waste Management Association
AWOIS	Automated Wreck and Obstruction Identification System (NOAA)
AWPI	American Wood Preservers Institute
AWQC	ambient water quality criteria, ambient water quality criterion

AWS	American Welding Society, available water capacity
AWT	advanced waste treatment
AWTF	advanced wastewater treatment facility
AWWA	American Water Works Association
AWWTP	advanced wastewater treatment plant
AWWU	Anchorage Water and Wastewater Utility
AZ	Arizona
B	concentration between detection limit and contract-required detection limit
B&PV Code	*Boiler and Pressure Vessel Code* (ASME document)
B&W	black and white (photograph)
B(a)P	benzo(a)pyrene
Ba	barium
BA	boric acid
BAAQMD	Bay Area Quality Management District (California)
BAC	blood alcohol concentration
BACT	best available control technology
BADCT	best available demonstrated control technology (Arizona)
BAE	bone acid evaporator
BAM	budget accounting management
BAN	base/acid/neutral
BASIC	Beginner's All-Purpose Symbolic Instruction Code (computer language)
BAST	boric acid storage tank
BATP	boric acid transfer pump
bbl	barrel
BCD	binary-coded decimal (noun)
BCF	bioconcentration factor
BCT	best conventional technology
BCW	bearing cooling water
BCWS	bearing cooling water system
BDAT	best demonstrated available technology (RCRA)
BDL	below detection limit
BDMT	bone dry metric ton
Be	beryllium
BEF	best-estimate flow
BETX	benzene, ethylbenzene, toluene, and total xylenes (use BTEX instead)
bgs	below ground surface
BHC	benzene hexachloride (insecticide)
BI	backward-inclined (adjective, e.g., BI fan)

BIA	Bureau of Indian Affairs
BIC	bearing identification code
BIF	boiler and industrial furnace
BIL	basic impulse level
BIST	boron injection surge tank
BIT	boron injection tank
BKR	breaker
BLDG	building
BLG	bulge
BLM	U.S. Bureau of Land Management
BLOB	Binary Large Object
BLPU	Basic Land and Property Unit
bls	barrels
BLS	black liquor solids; boundary layer separation
BLUE	Best Linear Unbiased Estimate
bmp	below the measuring point
BMP	Best Management Plan; best management practice
BMPP	Best Management Practices Plan
BNA	base, neutral, acid (extractables)
BOD	biochemical oxygen demand (an indicator of pollutant concentrations)
BOD_5	5-day biochemical oxygen demand (when preceded by "carbonaceous," use BOD instead)
BOL	beginning of (core) life
BOM	bill of materials
BOP	balance of plant
bp	boiling point
bpm	beats per minute
BPRA	burnable poison rod assembly
BPS	brazing procedure specification
BPXA	BP Exploration (Alaska) Inc.
BRC	below regulatory concern; bipolar relay converter
BRS	boron recovery system
BSU	Basic Spatial Unit
BTDC	before top dead center
BTEX	benzene, toluene, ethylbenzene, and total xylenes (preferred over BXTE or BETX)
BTP	*Branch Technical Position* (NRC document)
Btu	British thermal unit(s)
BTV	bleeder trip valve
BUECI	Barrow Utility Electric Cooperative, Inc.
BWR	boiling water reactor

BWT	Ballast Water Treatment
C of C	certificate of compliance
C	Celsius (Centrigrade is the International word)
C	slight change; control (interlock); coulomb; carbon; clay
C&D	construction and demolition (materials and waste)
C&RP	chemistry and radiation protection
C.E.	Civil Engineer
C.E.G.	Certified Engineering Geologist
C.S.E.	civil and sanitary engineer
C_6H_{14}	hexane
Ca	calcium; carcinogenic
CA	containment atmosphere, California; cellulose acetate
CAA	Clean Air Act
CAA(A)	Clean Air Act (Amendments)
CAAQS	California ambient air quality standard
CAB	cellulose acetate butyrate (McG-H0; Civil Aeronautics Board
CAC	containment air cooler; citizens' advisory committee
CACO	Corporate Administrative Contracting Officer
CACS	containment air cooler system
CAD	computer aided drafting, computer-aided design (use AutoCAD for the computer program)
CAD	computer-aided drafting, computer-aided design (I prefer CADD)
CADD	computer-aided drafting and design
CAE	computer-aided engineering, carbon alcohol extract
CAG	computer-aided graphics
CAL	computer-assisted learning
CAl	calibration
Cal-OSHA	California Occupational Safety and Health Administration
CAM	computer-aided mapping
CAM	continuous air monitor
CAP	corrective action program
CA-PASS	containment atmosphere-postaccident sampling system
CAPCOA	California Air Pollution Control Officers Association
CAR	corrective action request; corrective action report; closure action report, certified analytical report; contamination assessment report
CARC	chemical-agent-resistant coating
CAS	central alarm station; compressed air system; Chemical Abstracts Service (registry number), Columbia

	Analytical Services
CASE	computer-aided software engineering
CASE	coordinating agency for supplier evaluation
CBI	confidential business information
CBNS	Center for the Biology of Natural Systems
CBOA	cellobioseoctaacetate
CBOD5	carbonaceous 5-day biochemical oxygen demand
cc	obsolete--use cm^3 for cubic centimeter(s)
CCB	control center blower
CCC	calibration check compounds
cci	contact closure input, construction cost index
cco	contact closure output
CCP	centrifugal charging pump
CCR	*California Code of Regulations* (document)
CCRO	central control room operator
CCTV	closed-circuit television
CCU	central control unit
CCV	continuing calibration verification
CCW	component cooling water
ccw	counterclockwise
CCWE	constituent concentrations in the waste extract
ccws	component cooling water system
Cd	cadmium
CD	civil defense
CD&T	career development and training
CDC	Centers for Disease Control (HHS)
CDD/CDF	chlorinated dibenzo-p-dioxin and chlorinated dibenzofuran
CDE	chief discipline engineer
CDFG	California Department of Fish and Game
CDG	chlorine dioxide gas; chloride dioxide generating
CDI	chronic daily intake
CDL	Commercial Driver's License; construction, demolition, and land clearing
CDMG	California Division of Mines and Geology
CDMS	chemistry data management system
CDOG	California Division of Oil and Gas
CDQR	Chemical Data Quality Review
CE	combustion engineering
CEA	Chugach Electric Association
CEG	conditionally exempt generator
CEI	Chugach Engineering, Inc.; Central Environmental, Inc.

CEM	continuous emission monitoring
CEMS	continuos emission monitoring system
CEO	chief executive officer
CEQ	Council on Environmental Quality
CEQA	California Environmental Quality Act
CERB	Community Economic Revitalization Board
CERCLA	Comprehensive Environmental Response, Compensation, and Liability Act of 1980 (Superfund)
CERCLIS	Comprehensive Environmental Response, Compensation, and Liability Information System
CERI	Center for Environmental Research Information
CERNF	CERCLA Inventory Superfund Site/Event Listing subset (no further action at site required)
CESS	Control and Electrical Systems Standard (Westinghouse document)
CET	core exit thermocouple
CEU	continuing education unit
CFC	chlorofluorocarbon
cfd	obsolete—use ft^3 /day for cubic feet per day
CFI	cost, freight, and insurance
cfm	obsolete—use ft^3/minute for cubic feet per minute
CFPS	corporate financial planning system
CFR	*Code of Federal Regulations* (federal document); crash, fire, and rescue
CFS	core flooding system
cfs	obsolete—use ft^3 /second for cubic feet per second
CFT	core flooding tank
CGI	Common Gateway Interface
CGI	combustible-gas indicator
CGM	Computer Graphics Metafile
CH	chlorinated herbicide
CH4	methane
CHAS	containment hydrogen analysis system
CHEM	chemistry
CHG	charging
CHMM	Certified Hazardous Material Manager
CHRS	containment heat removal system
CHWDT	chemical waste drain tank
CHWMP	County Hazardous Waste Management Plan (California)
CHWS	chilled water system
CI	containment isolation
ci	curie(s)

CIB	containment isolation Phase B
CIC	compensated ionization chamber
CIDS	Concrete Island Drilling System
CIF	cost, insurance, and freight
CIH	Certified Industrial Hygienist; Certified Inshore Hydrographer
CIP	capital improvement program; cast-in-place; capital improvement project
CIS	containment isolation signal
CIV	combined intercept valve
CIWMB	California Integrated Waste Management Board (replaces California Waste Management Board)
CKD	cement kiln dust
CKT	circuit
CLI	contaminant level index
CLNG	cooling
CLP	Contract Laboratory Program (USEPA)
CLP-M	Contract Laboratory Program (modified)
CLV	concentration limit variance
cm	centimeter(s)
CM	construction management
cm/sec	centimeter(s) per second
cm³	cubic centimeter(s)
CMAA	Construction Management Association of America
CMAS	complete mix air-activated sludge
CMC	central monitoring and control
CMCB	centralized monitoring and control building
CMCF	centralized monitoring and control facility
CMD	corporate management document
CMEB	Chemical and Mechanical Engineering Branch (of the NRC)
CMI	corrective measures implementation
CMM	corporate management manual (type of document)
CMP	*Chemistry Manual* procedure; corrugated metal pipe
CMS	Construction Management Services; corrective management study; corrective measures study; compliance management system
CMTR	Certified Material Test Report (type of document)
CMU	concrete masonry unit
CN	cyanonaphthalene; cyanide
CNDSR	condenser

CNS	central nervous system
CNTRL	control
Co	cobalt
CO	contracting officer, control operator; Colorado; carbon monoxide
CO_2	carbon dioxide
COBOL	Common Business Oriented Language (computer language)
COC	chain of custody
COD	chemical oxygen demand; cash on delivery
COE	U.S. Army Corps of Engineers: use USACE for all references except Corps of Engineers documents—use COE. Subject to change.
COGO	coordinate geometry
COH	Certified Offshore Hydrographer
COM	Component Object Model; computer output microfilm; common
COMPLI	Compliance Information on Stationary Sources of Air Pollution (software)
COMPQAP	Comprehensive Quality Assurance Plan
COMPS	Computerized Operations and Maintenance Program System (software)
COMSAT	communications satellite
COR	contracting officer's representative
CORBA	Common Object Request Broker Architecture
CORS	continuously operating reference stations (used for GPS)
COSS	cost-of-service study
CP	cathodic protection
cp	centipoise(s)
CPAH	carcinogenic polycyclic (or polynuclear) aromatic hydrocarbon
CPF	cancer (or carcinogenic) potency factor
CPFF	cost plus fixed fee
CPI	Consumer Price Index
CPM	critical path method
cpm	cycle(s) per minute
CPP	chemical protection program
CPR	continuing property record; chemical purchase requisition, cardiopulmonary resuscitation
CPS	contour plotting system
cps	cycle(s) per second (synonym for hertz); count(s) per second

CPT	cone penetration test
CPU	central processing unit
CPUC	California Public Utilities Commission
CQA	construction quality assurance
CQC	construction quality control, contractor quality control
Cr	chromium
CR	control room
CRA	control rod assembly
CRDCS	control rod drive control system
CRDL	contract-required detection limit
CRDM	control rod drive mechanism
CRDS	control rod drive shaft
CRE	control room envelope
CRO	control room operator
CRP	Community Relations Plan
CRPD	control room pressure boundary
CRS	clean radwaste system; containment recirculation sump
CRT	cathode ray tube
CRWS	clean radioactive waste treatment system
Cs	cesium
CS	containment spray; commercial standard; chemical spray
CSA	channel statistical allowance
CSAS	containment spray actuation signal
CSB	Conversion Systems Branch (of the NRC)
CSC	company support center
CSD	cold shutdown (noun/adjective)
CSF	critical safety function
csf	cubic feet per second
CSFST	critical safety function status tree
CSI	Construction Specifications Institute; compliance sampling inspection (CWA); chemical substances inventory
CSIP	common stock investment plan
CSL	current switch logic; close support laboratory
CSLs	(marine sediment) cleanup screening levels
CSM	certified safety manager
CSO	combined sewer overflow
CSP	containment spray pump
CSR	cable spreading room
CSS	containment spray system; component summary sheet
CSSM	Content Standards for Spatial Metadata
CST	condensate storage tank

CSWMP	Comprehensive Solid Waste Management Plan
CT	current transformer; Connecticut
CTC	control technology center
CTD	conductivity, temperature, and depth
CTL	commitment tracking list
CTSS	computerized technical specification system
cu ft	obsolete—use ft^3 for cubic foot (or spell out)
cu yd	obsolete—use yd^3 for cubic yard (or spell out)
CU	channel uncertainty; consolidated-undrained; confining unit
Cu	copper
CU1	Confining Unit 1
CUB	citizens' utility board
CUP	conditional use permit
CV	control valve
CVAA	cold vapor atomic absorption
CVCS	chemical and volume control system
CVM	Client Value Model
CVT	constant voltage transformer
cw	clockwise
CWA	Clean Water Act (aka FWPCA)
CWIP	construction work in progress
CWM	chemical waste management
CWP	chemical work permit
CWRT	clean waste receiver tank
CWS	circulating water system
CY	calendar year
cy	cubic yard
cyc	cycle(s)
D	dead load (difference between hot and cold leg temperatures); drum; diluted sample
d	spell out day; penny (nail size)
D&DS	discharge and dilution stricture
DA	dose assessor; digital-to-analog (adjective, e.g., DA converter); discipline assistant
DAC	digital-to-analog- converter (hyphens per McG-H)
DAD	digital alarming dosimeter; dose assessment director
DAF	dissolved air flotation
dag	dekagram(s)
DAM	district administrative manager
DATS	diffused aeration treatment system
DB	database

dB	decibel
dB	decibel(s)
dBA	decibel (A-weighted scale)
DBA	design basis accident; doing business as; Davis-Bacon Act
DBE	design-basis earthquake; design-basis event
DBMS	Database Management System
DBP	disinfection by-product
DBRR	Design Basis Review Report (type of document)
DC	definite change; District of Columbia
DCA	dichloroethane
DCB	1,4-dichlorobenzene
DCD	Document Control Desk (of the NRC)
DCE	1,2-dichloroethane, 1,2-dichloroethene, dichloroethene
DCN	design change notice, drawing change notice
DCP	detailed construction package; design control package; design change package
DCR	design chance record
DCRDR	detailed control room design review
DDD	district discipline director; dichlorodiphenyldichloroethane
DDE	Dynamic Data Exchange
DDE	dichlorodiphenyldichloroethylene; dynamic data exchange
DDL	Data Definition Language
DDT	diesel day tank; 4, 4, dichlorodiphenyltrichloroethane
DE	Delaware, destruction efficiency
de	direct current
DEC	Department of Environmental Conservation (U.S.)
DECLG	double-ended cold leg guillotine
DEI	dose-equivalent iodine
DEIS	draft environmental impact statement (type of document)
DEM	Digital Elevation Model; Department of Emergency Management (Washington state agency)
DEMA	Diesel Engine Manufacturers Association
DEP	Department of Environmental Protection
DEPS	double-ended pump suction
DEQ	Department of Environmental Quality
DER	Department of Environmental Regulation
DERP/FUDS	Defense Environmental Restoration Program/Formerly Used Defense Sites

DEW-Line	Distant Early Warning Line (radar sites)
DF	decontamination factor; deflection factor; degree of freedom; deionization-filtration; dose factor; drive fit
DFO	diesel fuel oil
DFOS	diesel fuel oil system
DG	diesel generator
DGLS	diesel generator lubrication system
DGM	Digital Geospatial Metadata
DGPS	Differential Global Positioning System
DHHS	U.S. Department of Health and Human Services
DHRS	decay heat removal system
DHS	Department of Health Services (California)
DHSM	district health and safety manager
DHV	design hour volume
DI	demineralized; deionized; diluted; distilled; ductile iron
DID	direct inward dial
DIGEST	Digital Geographic Information Working Group Exchange Standard
DIME	Dual Independent Map Encoding
DIP	Digital Image Processing
DIR	design input record
DIW	deep injection well
DLC	donation land claim
DLCD	Department of Land Conservation and Development (of Oregon)
DLG	Digital Line Graph
DLRO	digital low-resistance ohmmeter ("ohmmeter" per McG-H)
DML	Data Manipulation Language
DMR	Discrepant Material Report (type of document)
DMW	deep monitor well
DNA	deoxyribonucleic acid
DNAPL	dense non-aqueous-phase liquid
DNB	departure from nucleate boiling
DNBR	departure from nucleate boiling ratio
DNR	Department of Natural Resources (Washington)
DO	delivery order, dissolved oxygen
DOC	Department of Commerce (federal department)
DOC	U.S. Department of Commerce
DOD	Department of Defense (federal department)
DOD	U.S. Department of Defense
DOE	U.S. Department of Energy; Department of Ecology (of

	Washington state)
DOGAMI	Oregon Department of Geology and Mineral Industries
DOI	U.S. Department of the Interior
DOJ	U.S. Department of Justice
DOL	U.S. Department of Labor (federal department)
DOR	Division of Operating Reactors (of the NRC)
DOS	Disk Operating System
DOT	U.S. Department of Transportation (federal department) (USDOT now preferred)
DOT&PF	Alaska Department of Transportation and Public Facilities
DP	differential pressure; delta pressure
DPAS	Defense Property Accountability System
DPD	N,N-diethyl-p-phenylenediaimine
DPI	dots per Inch
DPIS	differential pressure indicating switch
dpm	disintegration(s) per minute
DPM	district personnel manager
dps	disintegration(s) per second
DPST	double-pole single-throw (adjective)
DPT	dye penetration test
DPU	differential pressure unit
DPW	Department of Public Works
DQO	data quality objective
DRE	destruction and removal efficiency
DRF	discrepancy resolution form (type of document)
DRO	diesel range organics (don't add "s" to make plural)
DRP	discrete radioactive particle
DRPH	diesel-range petroleum hydrocarbons
DRPI	digital rod position indication; digital rod position indicating
DRR	Design Review Report (type of document)
DRW	dirty radioactive waste
DS	distorted indication; dissolved solids
DSHS	Department of Social and Health Services (Washington state agency)
DSI	direct-service industry
DSL	Division of State Lands (Oregon agency)
DT	delta temperature
dt	dry ton(s)
dt/day	dry tons per day
DTM	Digital Terrain Model

DTM	digital terrain model
DTO	danger tagged out
DTS	dedicated telephone system
DTSC	Department of Toxic Substances Control (California)
dv/dt	excessive fast-rising voltage wave fronts
DVM	digital voltmeter
DVMT	dirty waste drain tank
DW	dangerous waste
DWDI	double-width, double-inlet (adjective, e.g., DWDI fan)
DWI	deep well injection
DWMT	dirty waste monitor tank
DWPRF	dry weather peak-hour flow
DWR	Department of Water Resources (California, Idaho)
DWS	domestic water system
DWST	demineralized water storage tank
DXF	Digital Exchange Format
E	operating basis earthquake load; east
E. coli	*Escherichia coli*
EA	environmental allowance; Environmental Assessment
EAB	exclusion area boundary
EAD	energy-absorbing device
EADG	environmental assessment/dosimetry croup
EAF	electric arc furnace
EAL	emergency action level
EAP	employee assistance program; Emergency Action Plan
EB	equipment rinsate blank; equipment blank
EBCT	empty bed contact time
EBL	emergency battery lantern; emergency battery lighting; emergency battery licht
EBM	engineering branch manager
EBOP	emergency bearing oil pump
EBS	emergency broadcast system
EC	emergency coordinator; electrical conductivity; equivalent concentration
EC_{50}	concentration affecting 50 percent of organisms or producing a 50 percent reduction in a parameter
ECA	emergency contingency action
ECC	eccentricity; emergency command (or control) center
ECCS	emergency core cooling system
ECD	Environmental Cleanup Division, electron capture detection (detector)
ECI	essential control and instrumentation

ECL	Environmental Conservation Law
ECN	engineering change notice
Ecology	Department of Ecology (of Washington state)
ECP	estimated critical position (adjective, e.g., ECP calculation)
ECSIS	environmental cleanup site information system
EDA	Economic Development Administration
EDB	ethylene dibromide
EDC	ethylene dichloride
EDCN	engineering, design change notice
EDF	Environmental Defense Fund, electronic digital format;
EDG	emergency diesel generator
EDI	Electronic Data Interchange
EDIFACT	Electronic Data Interchange for Administration, Commerce and Transport
EDIP	Early Detection Incentive Program
EDMS	environmental database management system
EDNA	Environmental Designation for Noise Abatement
EDP	Electrical Department procedure; electronic data processing
EDTA	ethylenediaminetetraacetic acid, ethylene diamine triacetic acid
EDU	equivalent dwelling unit
EE	electrical engineer
EE/CA	engineering evaluation and cost analysis
EEEQ	electrical equipment environmental qualification
EEO	equal employment opportunity
EERI	Earthquake Engineering Research Institute
EERS	earth electrical resistivity survey
EFC	emergency fan cooler
EFF	E-field race
EFP	emergency fire procedure
EFPY	equivalent full-power year
EFSEC	Emergency Facility Site Evaluation Council (Washington state agency)
EFU-CG	exclusive farm use-crop grazing
Eh	oxidation-reduction potential (in millivolts)
EHC	electrohydraulic control
EHCS	electrohydraulic control system
EHF	extremely high frequency
EHR	electric hydrogen recombiner
EHRS	electric hydrogen recombiner system

EHS	environmental health and safety
EHV	extra-high voltage
EHW	extremely hazardous waste
EI	emergency instruction
EIA	Environmental Impact Assessment
EIC	Environmental Information Center
EIFOV	Effective Instantaneous Field of View
EIP	Emissions Inventory Plan
EIR	Environmental Impact Report (type of document)
EIS	Environmental Impact Statement (type of document) (NEPA)
ELD	extraction line drain
EM	electromagnetic; electromagnetometer
EMF	electric and magnetic field
emf	electromotive force
EMGY	emergency
EMI	electromagnetic interference
EMO	electric-motor-operated
EMP	electrical maintenance procedure; energy management program
EMSL	environmental monitoring and support laboratory
EMTIC	emission measurement technical information center
ENC	Electronic Navigation Chart
ENR CCI	*Engineering News-Record* construction cost index
ENR	*Engineering News-Record*
ENRAC	environmental remedial action
ENS	emergency notification system (NRC red phone)
EOB	end of business (day)
EOBC	Engineer Officer's Basic Course (U.S. Army Corps of Engineers)
EOC	emergency operations center
EOD	explosive ordnance disposal
EOF	emergency operations facility
EOP	emergency operating procedure
EOS	Earth Observation Satellite
EP	extreme pressure; emergency procedure; emergency plan; extraction procedure (EP toxicity test or criteria)
EPA	U.S. Environmental Protection Agency (USEPA preferred); electrical penetration assembly
EPC	emergency planning coordinator
EPCP	Emergency Preparedness and Contingency Plan
EPCRA	Environmental Planning Community Right-to-Know Act

EPDM	ethylene propylene diene monomer
EPI	emergency public information
EPR	ethylene propylene
EPRI	Electric Power Research Institute
EPS	effluent pumping station
EP$_{tox}$	toxicity (e.g., lead) evaluated in an extraction procedure
EPZ	emergency planning zone
EQ	equipment qualification; environmental qualification; ecological quotient
EQAG	equipment qualification advisory group
EQC	Environmental Quality Commission
EQDP	environmental qualification data package
EQS	equipment qualification summary
EQTR	equipment qualification test report
EQUIP	equipment
ER	event report; emergency response; electrical resistivity
ERB	engineering review board
ERC	energy resource center; emission reduction credit
ERDA	Energy Research Development Agency (once AEC; federal agency)
ERDS	emergency response data system
ERF	emergency response facility
ERG	emergency response guideline
ERIN	Environmental Resources Information Network
ERL	effects range low
ERM	effects range-medium values, emergency response manager
ERNS	Emergency Response Notification System (database)
EROS	Earth Resource Observation Systems
ERP	Emergency Response Plan
ERT	emergency response team (USEPA)
ERTS	Earth Resources Technology Satellite
ES	environmental stockpile
ESA	Environmental Site Assessment; Endangered Species Act
ESB	Environmental Services Branch (USEPA)
ESCI	Environmental Cleanup Site Information System (database) (replaced SDDB)
ESD	Environmental Sciences Department
ESEI	event-specific emergency instruction
ESF	engineered safety feature
ESFAS	engineered safety features actuation system

ESHB	engrossed d substitute house bill
ESI	environmental site investigation, expanded site investigation
ESP	electrostatic precipitator
ESP	electrostatic precipitator; exchangeable sodium percentage
E-Spec	Equipment specification
ESR	electron spin resonance
ESRI	Environmental Systems Research Institute (developers of ArcInfo)
ET	elevated temperature; evapotranspiration; effective temperature; emergency tank; electronic transfer
ETS	environmental technical specification; emergency trip system; east tank farm
eV	electron volt
EVA	early valve actuation
EWTS	expandable wing tank structure
EXH	exhaust
F	farad; fluoride; flyash
F⁻	fluoride ion
FAA	Federal Aviation Administration; flame atomic absorption (spectrophotometry)
fab	fabrication facility
FAC	facilities associate contractor; factor; farm advisory committee; fast as can; field accelerator; final acceptance criterion-, fixed air capacitor; free available chlorine; frequency analysis and control
FAQ	Frequently Asked Question
FAR	Federal Acquisition Regulation
FARR	facility assessment risk reduction
FB	freight bill; field blank
FBI	Federal Bureau of Investigation (federal bureau)
fbm	board foot; board foot measure
FC	flow controller; fecal coliform; field capacity
fc	foot candle(s)
FCC	Federal Communications Commission
FCD	fluid cooler drain (adjective, e.g., FCD header)
FCN	field change notice; fuel change notice
FCS	field control sample; facility control system
FCU	flow control unit
FCV	flow control valve
FD	feed; fire departments; free dock; field duplicate

FDA	U.S. Food and Drug Administration
FDDI	Fiber Distributed Data Interface
FDER	Florida Department of Environmental Regulation
FDM	frequency deviation meter; functional development model; feasibility demonstration model; formal development method
FDR	feeder
FE	flow element
Fe	iron
FEA	Federal Energy Administration
FEIS	final environmental impact statement (type of document)
FEMA	Federal Emergency Management Agency (not Association or Administration)
FERC	Federal Energy Regulatory Commission
FET	field-effect transistor
FFA	full freight allowed; federal facilities agreement (type of contract)
FFCA	federal facilities compliance agreement
FFD	fitness for duty
FFP	firm fixed price
FGCC	Federal Geodetic Control Committee
FGDC	Federal Geographic Data Committee
FH	fuel handling
FHA	Federal Housing Administration; fire hazards analysis
FHP	fuel-handling procedure
FHWA	Federal Highway Administration
FI	flow indicator
FIC	flow-indicating controller
FICA	Federal Insurance Contributions Act
FID	flame ionization detection; flame ionization detector
FIFRA	Federal Insecticide, Fungicide, and Rodenticide Act
FINDS	Facility Index System (database)
FIPS	Federal Information Processing Standard
	fire-resistant (adjective, e.g., FR items)
FIS	flow-indicating switch; *Flood Insurance Study* (document)
FIT	field investigation team
FIT	flow-indicating transmitter
FJS	fluid jet supply
FL	full length; Florida
FLAM	flammable
FLMC	full-load motor current

fm	fentometer(s)
FM	frequency modulation; flowmeter
FmHA	Farmers' Home Administration
FML	flexible material liner, flexible membrane liner
FMP	Facilities Management Plan
FMP	Fisheries (or Fishery) Management Plan
FO	free oil
FOB	free on board
FODP	Fuel Operations Department procedure
FOG	fat, oil, and grease
FONSI	finding of no significant impact
fp	fire protection; freezing point
FPIC	fire protection interface control
fpm	flash(es) per minute; feet per minute; foot per minute
FPS	fire protection system
fps	flash(es) per second; feet per second; foot per second
FR	flow recorder; functional restoration; *Federal Register* (document);
FRC	federal response center
FRG	fully regulated generator
FRI	functional restoration instruction, focused remedial investigation
FRMAC	Federal Radiological Monitoring and Assessment Center
FRPA	Fixed Radiation Pattern Antenna
FRRP	Federal Radiological Response Plan (type of document)
FRSTDOSE	computer code for initial dose assessment
FS	Feasibility Study; factor of safety
FS/RA	Feasibility Study/Risk Assessment
FSAP	Field Sampling and Analysis Plan
FSAR	Final Safety Analysis Report (type of document)
FSP	Field Sampling Plan (type of document)
FSPF	first-stage pressure feedback
FSRA	Full-Service Remedial Action
FST	fuel storage tank
FT	flow transmitter
ft	use for foot only in table/graph/equation, if space tight
ft^2	square foot or square feet or sq ft
FTA	field termination assembly; Federal Transit Administration
FTC	field team coordinator
FTE	full-time equivalent
FTL	field team leader

FTP	file transfer protocol
FTS	fuel transfer system
FUDS	formerly used defense site
FVNR	full-voltage nonreversing (adjective, e.g., FVNR controller)
FVR	full-voltage reversing (adjective, e.g., FVR controller)
FW	feedwater
FWD	falling weight deflectometer
FWHM	full width at half the maximum (adjective, e.g., FWHM peak height)
FWI	feedwater isolation
FWIS	feedwater isolation signal
FWIV	feedwater isolation valve
FWPCA	Federal Water Pollution Control Act (aka CWA)
FWQCs	federal water quality criteria
FWRV	feedwater regulating valve
FWS	fire water system
FY	fiscal year
FYI	for your information
G	gauss (magnetic field strength); giga (10^9 prefix), acceleration (14g vertical); gram(s)
g/sec	gram(s) per second
GA	Georgia
GAC	granular activated carbon
gal.	use for "gallon(s)" only in table/graph/equation, if space tight
GAM	Geographical Analysis Machine
GAO	General Accounting Office (federal office)
GBF/DIME	Geographic Base File/Dual Independent Map Encoding
GBT	gravity-belt thickener
GC	gas chromatograph; gas chromatography
GC/MS	gas chromatography/mass spectrometry
GCH	gas collection header
GDT	gas decay tank
GDTDP	gas decay tank discharge permit
GE	general emergency; General Electric Company
GEIS	generic environmental impact statement
GEOSAT	Geodetic Satellite
GEP	good engineering practice
GET	general employee training
GFAA	graphite furnace atomic absorption
GFCI	ground fault circuit interrupter

GFI	ground fault indicator; round fault interrupter
GIRAS	Geographic Information Retrieval and Analysis
GIS	Geographic Information System
GKS	Graphics Kernel System
GL	class containers
GLA	generation licensing and analysis
GLONASS	Global Navigation Satellite System
GLPC	gas-liquid partition chromatography
GM	gas monitor; general manager
GMAW	gas-metal arc welding (MIG welding)
GMT	Greenwich Mean Time
GNP	gross national product
GO	government obligation (bond type)
GOES	Geostationary Operational Environmental Satellite
GOI	general operating instruction
gpapd	gallon(s) per acre per day
gpcpd	gallon(s) per capita per day
gpd	gallon(s) per day
gpd/ft	gallons per day per foot
gpm	gallon(s) per minute
GPO	Government Printing Office (federal office)
GPR	ground-penetrating radar
gps	gallon(s) per second
GPS	Global Positioning System
gr/dscf	grain(s) per dry standard cubic foot
GRASS	Geographic Resources Analysis Support System
GRO	gasoline range organics (don't add "s" to GRO to make plural)
GRPH	gasoline-range petroleum hydrocarbon
GRS	ground radio system; gaseous radiologic waste system
GRW	gaseous radwaste
GSA	Geological Society of America; General Services Administration (U.S.)
GT	gas team
GTAW	gas tungsten arc welding (TIG welding)
GTG	gas turbine generator
GU	general utility
GUI	Graphical User Interface
GW	groundwater; gas well
GWP-Ind	groundwater protection standard(s) for industrial use
GWT	gross weight
H	henry (inductance unit)

H&S	health and safety
H&TMH	hazardous and toxic materials handling (facility)
H&V	heating and ventilation
H:V	horizontal:vertical (slope)
H_2O	water
H_2S	hydrogen sulfide
H_2SO_3	sulfurous acid
H_2SO_4	sulfuric acid
HA	health advisory; health and safety
HAA	haloacetic acid
HAD	heat-actuated detector
HAP	hazardous air pollutant; hydroxylamine perchlorate
HAR	Hydrogeologic Assessment Report
HARL	high airborne radioactivity level
HARN	High Accuracy Reference Network
HAS	hollow-stem auger
HASP	Health and Safety Plan
HAZMAT	hazardous materials
HAZWOPER	Hazardous Waste Operations and Emergency Response
HB	house bill (e.g., House Bill 247)
HBHC	high-boiling-point hydrocarbons
HCDT	hard-copy data transmission; hard-copy data transmitter; hard-copy data terminal
HCl	hydrochloric acid; hydrogen chloride
HCID	hydrocarbon identification
HCRF	Hydrographic Chart Raster Format
HCV	hand control valve
HDAPS	The Hydrographic Data Acquisition and Processing System
HDCS	Hydrographic Data Cleaning Software
HDP	heater drain pump
HDPE	high-density polyethylene
HDR	header
HDT	hard-copy data transmission; heater drain tank
HECL	harsh environmental current leakage
HED	human engineering deficiency; human engineer-in-discrepancy
HELB	high-energy line break
HELP	hydrologic evaluation of landfill performance (model)
HEPA	high-efficiency particulate air (adjective, e.g., HEPA filter)
HF	high frequency; heavy fuel; hundred feet; hydrogen

	fluoride; hollow
HFP	hot full power
Hg	mercury
HgA	air (atmospheric) pressure
HGL	hydraulic grade level
HH	halogenated hydrocarbon
HHW	hazardous household waste
HI	hazard index
HIRL	high-intensity runway light
HMIS	hazardous materials inventory statement
HMO	health maintenance organization
HMS	hydrogen mixing system
HMTA	Hazardous Materials Transportation Act (1974, 1990)
H_o	pipe reactions under normal operating conditions
HOC	halogenated organic compound
HOV	high-occupancy vehicle
HP	high-pressure (adjective); Hewlett Packard
hp	horsepower
HPES	human performance evaluation system
HPF	high power factor
hp-hr	horsepower-hour
HPI	high-pressure injection
HPL	hurricane protection level
HPLC	high-performance liquid chromatography
HPM	hazardous production material
HQ	hazard quotient
hr	use for hour only in table/graph/equation, if space tight
HRCQ	highway route controlled quantity
HRS	hazard ranking system
HRSG	heat recovery steam generator
HRV	High Resolution Visible
HS	hand switch
HSB	hot standby (noun/adjective)
HSD	hot shutdown (noun/adjective)
HSHSG	hazardous and contaminated substance health and safety guide
HSM	health and safety manager
HSMS	Hazardous Substances Management System
HSP	Health and Safety Plan (type of document); also see SHP
HSWA	Hazardous and Solid Waste Amendments
HTGR	high-temperature gas-cooled reactor
HTM	high-trajectory missile

HTMR	high-temperature metal recovery
HTRW	hazardous, toxic or radioactive waste
HTTP	Hypertext Transfer Protocol
HTU	height of transfer unit
HTW	hazardous toxic waste
HUD	U.S. Department of Housing and Urban Development
HUT	hold-up tank
HV	high-voltage (adjective, e.g., HV unit)
HVAC	heating, ventilation, and air conditioning (compound noun)
HVDC	high-voltage direct current
HVE	high vacuum extraction
HWDF	hazardous-waste-derived fuel
HWDMS	Hazardous Waste Data Management System (OSWER)
HWIS	Hazardous Waste Information System
HWMP	Hazardous Waste Management Plan
HX	heat exchanger
HYD	hydraulic
Hz	hertz
HZP	hot zero power
I	iodine
I&C	instrumentation and control
I.D.	identification
i.d.	inside diameter
I/I	infiltration and inflow
I/O	input/output (adjective, e.g., I/O device)
I/P	electropneumatic (adjective, e.g., I/P converter)
I/V	current/voltage (adjective, e.g., I/V input)
IA	instrument air; Iowa
IAC	Inter-application Communication
IAEA	International Atomic Energy Agency
IAH	International Association of Hydrogeologists
IARC	International Agency for Research on Cancer
IAW	in accordance with
IBD	isolated bus duct; (cooler) isolated (phase) bus duct
IBEW	International Brotherhood of Electrical Workers
IC	ion chromatography
IC(A)P	inductively coupled (argon) plasma
IC_{25}	concentration causing a 25 percent reduction in biological growth
ICA	independent cost assessment; instrument control and automation; investigative and corrective action; ionized

	calcium analyzer
ICBO	International Conference of Building Officials
ICC	inadequate core cooling; (U.S.) Interstate Commerce Commission
ICEA	Insulated Cable Engineers Association
ICP	instrumentation and control procedure; inductively coupled plasma; internal communication plan, interim cleanup plan
ICRP	International Commission on Radiological Protection
ICRPM	International Commission on Radiation Protection and Measurement
ICRU	International Commission on Radiological Units
ICS	integrated control system; industrial control standard
ICSB	Instrumentation and Control Systems Branch (of the NRC)
ICU	copper indication
ICV	individual cell voltage
ID	Idaho
IDA	International Development Association
IDB	industrial development bond
IDCN	interim design chance notice; interim drawing chan-e notice
IDF	intensity-duration-frequency
IDIQ	indefinite delivery/indefinite recovery
IDL	instrument detection limit
IDLH	immediately dangerous to life and health
IDO	indefinite delivery order
IDTC	Indefinite Delivery Type Contract
IDTRA	Indefinite Delivery Type Remedial Action
IDU	intertie development and use
IDUG	interdepartmental users' group
IDV	inside diameter variation
IDW	investigation-derived waste
IDWR	Idaho Department of Water Resources
IE	Office of Inspection and Enforcement (of the NRC)
IEEE	Institute of Electrical and Electronics Engineers
IEIN	inspection and enforcement information notice (type of NRC document)
IEIR	Inspection and Enforcement Inspection Report (type of NRC document)
IES	Illuminating Engineering Society
IF	intermediate frequency

IFB	invitation for bids
IFIM	instream flow incremental methodology
IFMA	International Facility Management Association
IFOV	Instantaneous Field of View
IFR	instrument flight rule
IGDS	Interactive Graphics Design Software
IGES	International Graphics Exchange System
IGSL	industrial-grade suppliers list
IHMM	Institute of Hazardous Materials Management
IHO	International Hydrographic Organization
IHP	in-house position
IL	indicating light; Illinois
ILM	frequency control unit
ILRT	integrated leak rate test
ILS	instrument landing system
IMB	inside missile barrier
IMF	International Monetary Fund
IMP	information management procedure
IMPATT	impact ionization avalanche transient time
IMS	in-core monitoring system
IMU	Inertial Measurement Unit
in.	use for inch only in table/graph/equation, if space tight
INM	indication not measurable
IO	ion exchanger
IOS	inventory ordering system
IOU	investor-owned utility; I owe you
IP	information processing; inspection plan
IPE	individual plant examination
IPL	initial pressure limiter
IPS	iron pipe size
IQR	interquartile range
IR	infrared
IR	intermediate range; infrared resistance; insulation resistance; infrared radiation
IRA	interim remedial action
IRAP	Interim Remedial Action Plan
IRDS	Information Resource Dictionary System
IRIS	Infrared Interferometer Spectrometer
IRIS	Integrated Risk Information System
IRM	Interim Remedial Measures (CERCLA)
IRP	*Nuclear Incident Response Plan* (NUREG-0728. an NRC document), radium dial painter; Installation

	Restoration Program
IRS	infrared spectroscopy; Internal Revenue Service (federal agency)
IRTS	Infrared Temperature Sounder
IS	installation standard
ISA	Instrument Society of America
ISAS	instrument and service air system
ISBN	International Standard Book Number
ISC	initial site characterization
ISCA	isolator calibration accuracy
ISCST	industrial source complex-short term (EPA model)
ISD	isolator drift
ISDN	Integrated Services Digital Network
ISI	in-service inspection
ISIS	Inflatable Sunshield in Space
ISM	Interstellar Medium
ISO	International Standards Organization
ISOL	isolation
ISS	*Interim Status Standards* (document)
IST	in-service testing
ITDP	improved thermal design procedure
IV	intercept valve
IW	industrial wastewater
IWT	industrial waste treatment; integrated wastewater treatment
J	joule; estimated value; estimated result
JAR	job approval request
JCO	justification for continued operation
JE	journal entry
JEIP	joint emissions inventory program
JFA	jurisdictional flow agreement (type of contract)
JPEG	Joint Photographic Expert Group
JRG	job review group
JTU	Jackson turbidity unit
k	kilo
K	kelvin, unit of thermodynamic temperature; potassium; hydraulic conductivity (ft/sec); estimated result (biased high)
kbps	kilobits per second
keV	kileoelectron volt(s)
kg	kilogram(s)
kg/ha	kilogram(s) per hectare

kg/L	kilogram(s) per liter
kHz	kilohertz
KI	potassium iodide
kip	unit of weight equal to 1,000 pounds, used to express deadweight load
kJ	kilojoule (energy measure)
km	kilometer
KPEG	potassium hydroxide/polyethylene glycol
KS	Kansas
ksf	kips (thousands of pounds) per square foot
kV	kilovolt(s)
kVA	kilovolt-ampere(s)
kW	kilowatt(s)
kWh	kilowatt-hour
KY	Kentucky
L	live load; liter; length of screened interval in feet; lagoon;
l	see L
L&I	Department of Labor and Industries (Washington)
L/O	locked out
LA	Louisiana
LAER	lowest achievable emission rate
LAN	Local Area Network
Landsat	Land Remote Sensing Satellite
LANL	Los Alamos National Laboratory
LANT	local area network
LAP	laboratory analytical protocol
lat	latitude
lb	pound(s)
LC	level controller; load center (of switchgear); locked closed; lower clay
lc	lowercase (i.e., not capitalized)
LC_{50}	lethal concentration with 50 percent mortality
LCA	license chance application
LCC	load control center
LCL	lower control limit
LCM	large core memory
LCO	limiting condition for operation
LCR	license change request; license change report
LCRS	leachate collection and removal system
LCS	local control station; laboratory control sample
LCSC	laboratory control sample duplicate

LCU	load control unit
LCV	level control valve
LD50	lethal dose for 50 percent of a population
LDCR	licensing document change request
LDCRS	leachate detection collection, and removal system
LDI	licensing document interpretation
Ldn	weighted forecast of airport noise exposure level
LDPE	low-density polyethylene
LDR	land disposal restriction
LEA	local enforcement agency
LED	light-emitting diode
LEL	lower explosive limit; lower exposure limit
LER	Licensee Event Report (type of document)
LET	linear energy transfer
LEW	leachate extraction well
LFG	landfill gas
LFL	lower flammability limit
LI	level indicator, liquidity index
Li	lithium
LIC	level-indicating controller
LID	local improvement district
LIDAR	Light Detection and Ranging
lin ft	linear foot; linear feet
LIS	Land Information System
LIS	level-indicating switch; licensing information service
LIT	level-indicating transmitter
LL	liquid limit
LLC	Limited Liability Company
LLD Report	Lower Limit of Detection Report (type of document)
LLD	lower-level discriminator; lower limit of detection
LLEA	local law enforcement agency
LLRT	local leak rate test
lm	lumen; lumina
LMTD	log mean temperature difference
LN	line
ln	natural logarithm
LN_2	liquid nitrogen
LNAPL	light non-aqueous-phase liquid
LNG	liquefied natural gas
L_O	equivalent live load
LOA	local operation action; local operator action
LOAEL	lowest observable adverse effects level; lowest observed

	adverse effect level
LOCA	loss-of-coolant accident
LOD	limit of detection
LOEP	list of effective passes
LOQ	limit (level) of quantification
LOS	level of service
LOSC	loss of secondary coolant
LP	low pressure (noun); low-pressure (adjective, e.g., LP turbine); loop; line printer
LPAH	polycyclic aromatic hydrocarbon
LPEC	local peripheral entry controller
LPG	liquefied petroleum gas
LPIS	low-pressure injection system
LPMA	loose parts monitoring system
LPO	local purchase order
LPP	loss prevention program
LPPS	lighting panel power supply
LPR	liquid penetration rate
LPST	leaking petroleum storage tank
LPT	liquid penetration test
LR	level recorder
LRC	lead resistance compensator; level recording controller; line rectifier circuit
LRRS	Long Range Radar Site
LRT	light rail transit
LS	level switch; line segment, lump sum
LSA	low Specific activity
LSSS	limiting safety system setting
LT	level transmitter-, locked throttled
LTDN	letdown (noun/adjective)
LTM	low-trajectory missile
LTO/LTM	long-term operations/long-term maintenance
LTOPS	low-temperature overpressure system
LUFT	leaking underground fuel tank
LUT	Look-up Table
LW	lower waste
LXDA	linear x-ray detector array
m	meter; milli
M&TE	measuring and test equipment
MΩ	megohm(s)
M/SR	material/service request
MA	Massachusetts

mA	milliampere(s)
MACE	Material Association of Corrosion Engineers
MACRO	(a system control computer language)
MACT	maximum achievable control technology
Maint	maintenance
MAPS	Mesoscale Analysis and Prediction System
MAWP	maximum average working pressure
mb	millibar
MBA	Metropolitan Business Association, master's of business administration
MBE	minority business enterprise (designation)
Mbps	megabits per second
MBWA	management by wandering around
Mbyte	megabyte
MCA	multichannel analyzer
MCAC	management corrective action committee
MCES	main condenser evacuation system
MCL	maximum contaminant level
MCLG	maximum contaminant level goal
MCM	circular mils, in thousands (a cable size); thousand circular mils; million cubic meters; mercury cycling model
MCP	maximum permissible concentration
MCPA	methylchlorophenoxyacetic acid (a herbicide)
MCPWR	microcomputer model for dynamic analysis of pressurized water reactor plants
MCS	master control switch; model conservation standard
MD	Maryland
MDA	minimum detectable activity
MDC	mechanical design criterion
MDD	maximum day demand
MDF	mechanical design flow
MDL	method detection limit
MDS	makeup demineralizer system
MDSR	material disposal and sales request
ME	Maine
MEE	material engineering evaluation
MEK	methyl ethyl ketone
MELB	moderate-energy line break
meq	milliequivalent(s)
MET	scrap metals
METEOSAT	Geosynchronous Meteorology Satellite (ESA)

MeV	mega electron volts
MeV	megaelectron volt(s)
MF	medium frequency
MFS	Minimum Functional Standards for Solid Waste Handling (Washington)
MFT	materials functional task
MFW	main feedwater (adjective, e.g., MFW pump)
MFWLB	main feedwater line break
MFWP	main feedwater pump
Mg	magnesium
mg	milligram(s)
MG	motor generator; million gallon(s)
mg/kg	milligram(s) per kilogram (some companies prefer mg/Kg)
mg/L	milligram(s) per liter
mgd	million gallon(s) per day
MH	manhole; silt with clay
MHD	magnetohydrodynanuc; maximum hour demand
MHHW	mean higher high water
mht	mean high tide
MHW	mean high water
MHWL	mean high water line
MHz	megahertz
mHz	millihertz
MI	mineral insulated (adverb); mineral-insulated (adjective, e.g., MI equipment); Michigan
MIBK	4-methyl-2-pentanone
MIG	metal-inert gas (kind of underwater welding; see GMAW entry)
millirem	milliroentgen equivalent man
MIL-STD	Military Standard (federal document section)
min	use for minute only in table/graph/equation, if space tight
MIS	management information system
MIT	mechanical integrity testing
ml	milliliter(s)
MLD	maximum lethal dose
MLLW	mean lower low water
MLO	main lube oil
MLSS	mixed-liquor suspended solids
MLW	mean low water
mm	millimeter(s)

mM	millimolar (concentration, e.g., 2 mM nitrogen)
MMD	maximum month demand
MMDS	maximum-month dry-season (adjective)
MMDW	maximum-month dry-weather (adjective)
MMF	magnetomotive force
mmol	milllmole(s) (mass, e.g., 2 mmol of the substance)
MMPA	Marine Mammal Protection Act
MMSW	mixed municipal solid waste
MMWS	maximum-month wet-season (adjective)
Mn	manganese
MN	Minnesota
MO	motor-operated (adjective, e.g., MO device); Missouri
mo.	use for month only in table/graph/equation, if space tight
MOA	Municipality of Anchorage,multiple-objective amenity
MODEM	modulate-demodulate
MODT	modified oven drying technique
MOGAS	motor gasoline
MOP	mixed other paper; monitoring only plan
MORT	management oversight and risk- tree
MOU	Memorandum of Understanding
MOV	motor-operated valve
MP	maintenance procedure; Mile point
mp	melting point
MPA	Office of Management and Program Analysis (NRC office)
MPBB	maximum permissible body burden
MPC	maximum permissible concentration
MPD	maximum permissible dose
MPI	maintenance pickup item
MPN	most probable number (bacteria count)
MPS	makeup and purification system
MR	master relay; maintenance request
mR	milliroentgen(s)
M_r	resilient modulus
MRB	material review board
MRF	material recovery facility
MRFF	maximum required fire flow
MRG	management review group
MRL	method reporting limit; method reporting level
MRO	medical review officer
MRW	moderate-risk waste
MS	Mississippi; mass spectrometry; matrix spike

MS/MSD	matrix spike/matrix spike duplicate
MSAC	mitigation system actuation circuitry
MSB	Matanuska-Susitna Borough
MSC	*Mechanical Specialty Code* (document); media-specific concentration
MSD	matrix spike duplicate
MSDS	Material Safety Data Sheet
MSE	mechanically stabilized earth
MSHA	Mine Safety and Health Administration
MSIV	main steam isolation valve
MSL	mean sea level
msl	mean sea level (e.g., 54 feet above the msl)
MSLB	main stream line break
MSLI	main stream line isolation
MSP	motor suction pump
MSPR	material/service purchase requisition
MSR	moisture separator reheater; main steam relief
MSRV	main steam relief valve
MSS	Multispectral Scanner
MSS	main steam supply; Manufacturers Standardization Society; Material Standards Society
MSSS	main steam support structure
MSV	mean square voltage
MSW	municipal solid waste
MSWLF	municipal solid waste landfill
MT	magnetic (particle) test; Montana
mt	mean tide
MTBE	methyl-tert-butylether
MTBF	mean time between failures
MTR	Material Test Report (type of document)
MTSV	master trip solenoid valve
MTU	magnetic tape unit
MTVS	mechanical trip valve switch
MU	mapping unit
MUD	municipal utility district
MUPP	makeup pump
MUTCD	*Manual of Uniform Traffic Control Devices* (document)
mV	millivolt(s)
MVA	megavolt ampere(s)
mVA	millivolt ampere(s)
MW	megawatt(s); monitoring well
mW	milliwatt(s)

mwh	mean high water
mwl	mean water line
MWP	mixed waste paper
MWTS	makeup water treatment system
N	north; newton(s); spike sample recovery not within control limits
N'IP	National Toxicology Program
N0₃	nitrate
N₂	nitrogen
NA	not applicable; not authorized; not available; not analyzed (some companies prefer N/A for not applicable)
Na	sodium
NAAQS	national (primary and secondary) ambient air quality standard(s)
NACE	National Association of Corrosion Engineers
NaCO₃	soda ash
NAD	North American Datum
NAF	Naval Air Field
NAHB	National Association of Home Builders
NAMA	National Agricultural Marketing Association
NAOH	liquid caustic soda
NAPL	non-aqueous-phase liquid
NAPP	National Aerial Photography Program
NARUC	National Association of Regulatory Utility Commissioners
NAS	National Academy of Sciences
NASA	National Aeronautics and Space Administration
NASCOM	NASA Communications Network
NASD	Nuclear Administrative Services Department
NASDP	Nuclear Administrative Services Department procedure
NATICH	National Air Toxics Information Clearinghouse *National Standard* (document)
NATLSCO	National Loss Control Service Corporation-
NAV D88	North American Vertical Datum of 1988
NAVO	National Oceanographic Office
NAWAS	national warning system
NAX	ion-exchange softening
NBC	*National, Building Code* (document)
NBIC	*National Board Inspection Code* (document)
NBS	National Bureau of Standards
NC	no change; North Carolina; not calculated

NCAR	Nonconformance Activity Report (type of document)
NCARB	National Council of Architectural Registration Board (in D.C.)
NCASI	National Council for Air and Stream Improvement
NCDC	National Climatic Data Center
NCIC	National Cartographic Information Center
NCL	National Chemical Laboratory
NCN	nonconforming notice
NCP	*National Contingency Plan,* also known as *National Oil and Hazardous Substances Pollution Contingency Plan* (document)
NCR	Nonconformance Report (type of document)
NCRP	National Council on Radiation Protection
NCRPM	National Council on Radiation Protection and Measurement (once Advisory Committee on X-Ray and Radium Protection)
ND	North Dakota; not detected above detection limit; not detected
NDE	nondestructive examination
NDT	northeast, Nebraska
NEC	*National Electrical Code* (MCG-H/NEC handbook); Nuclear Energy Commission
NEDCO	Neighborhood Economic Development Corporation
NEIC	National Enforcement Investigations Center (OEC)
NELL	Nuclear Electric Insurance, Limited
NELPA	Northwest Electric Light and Power Association
NEL-PIA	Nuclear Energy Liability-Property Insurance Association
NEMA	National Electrical Manufacturers Association
NEP	National Estuaries Program
NEPA	National Environmental Policy Act
NEPIA	Nuclear Energy Property Insurance Association
NERA	National Economic Research Association
NERC	National Electric Reliability Council
NESC	*National Electrical Safety Code* (document)
NESCO	Northwest Energy Services Company
NESHAP	National Emission Standards for Hazardous Air Pollutants
NEW	Nuclear Energy Women
NFA	no further action
NFC	*National Fire Code* (document)
NFPA	National Fire Protection Association
NFRAP	no further response action planned

NFS	Network File System
NGD	National GeoSpatial Database
NGS	National Geodetic Survey (U.S.)
NH	New Hampshire
NH_3	ammonia
NH_3-N	ammonia-nitrogen
NHD	National Hydrography Dataset (USEPA and USCG)
Ni	nickel
NIH	National Institutes of Health
NIMA	National Image and Mapping Agency
NIN	Northwest Irrigation Network
NIOSH	National Institute of Occupational Safety and Health
NIS	nuclear instrumentation system
NIST	National Institute of Standards and Technology
NJ	New Jersey
NL	no limit found in literature
NLA	net feasible area
NLGI	National Lubricating Grease Institute
NLIS	National Land Information Service
NLRB	National Labor Relations Board
nm	nanometer(s)
NM	New Mexico; no measurement
NMAC	Nuclear Maintenance Applications Center (of the EPRI)
NMCs	nine minimum controls
NMD	number mean diameter (of particles)
NMFS	National Marine Fisheries Service
NMPX	nonmultiplexed
NMSS	Nuclear Material Safety and Standards (NRC office)
NNC	Northway Native Corporation
NNM	nuclear magnetic resonance
NNRIPA	National Nuclear Risks Insurance Pools and Associations
NNS	nonnuclear safety
NO_2	nitrogen dioxide
NO_3	notrogen oxide
NOAA	National Oceanic and Atmospheric Administration (under the U.S. Department of Commerce)
NOAEL	no observed adverse effect level; no observable adverse effect level
NOB	Nuclear Operations Board (of the NRC)
NOC	notice of construction (e.g., an NOC issue)
NOD	notice of deficiency (RCRA); notice of disposal

	(Arizona)
NOEC	no observable effect concentration; no observed effect concentration
NOI	notice of intent
NON	notice of noncompliance
non-QA	non-quality-assurance (adjective, e.g., non-QA issue)
NOR	normal
NOS	National Ocean Service (part of NOAA)
NOSC	Naval Ocean Systems Center
NOV	notice of violation (from NRC)
NO_x	nitrogen oxides
NPAR	nuclear plant aging research
NPB	Nuclear Regulation Branch
NPDES	National Pollutant Discharge Elimination System
NPDL	National Pacific Division Laboratory
NPL	National Priorities List (note plural Priorities)
NPM	net profit margin
NPPC	Northwest Power Planning Council
NPR	new production reactor
NPRDS	nuclear plant reliability data system
NPS	National Park Service
NPS	Nuclear Power Services (Westinghouse division); National Park
NPSH	net positive suction head
NPTF	national pipe tight fit
NPV	net present value
NQ	non-quality-related (adjective/adverb)
NQA	nuclear quality assurance
NR	not requested; not required; narrow range
NRC	Nuclear Regulatory Commission (federal agency)
NRCIRC	NRC Incident Response Center (Bethesda center)
NRCOC	NRC Operations Center (headquarters)
NRCS	Natural Resource Conservation Service
NRDA	natural resource damage assessment
NRF	northwest regional forecast
NRL	Naval Research Laboratory
NRMCA	National Ready-Mixed Concrete Association
NRR	Nuclear Reactor Regulation (NRC office)
NRS	nonrising steam
NS	not sampled
NSAC	Nuclear Safety Analysis Center (NRC center)
NSB	North Slope Borough

NSC	Nuclear Services Corporation; National Security, Council
NSD	normal shutdown (noun); Nuclear Security Department
NSF	National Science Foundation; National Sanitation Foundation
NSH	*National Soils Handbook* (document)
NSIC	Nuclear Safety Information Center
NSP	nuclear security procedure
NSPS	National Society of Professional Land Surveyors
NSR	new source review
NSRI	nuclear safety and regulation instruction
NSRP	nuclear safety and regulation procedure
NSS	nuclear steam system
NSSS	nuclear steam supply system
NSWMA	National Solid Waste Management Association
NSY	naval shipyard
nT	nano-Tesla
NT	Northwest Territories
NTF	National Tranfer Format
NTIS	National Technical Information Service
NTS	not to scale (used in figures)
NTU	nephelometric turbidity unit
NUCON	Nuclear Consulting Services, Inc.
NUFPG	Nuclear Utility Fire Protection Group (utilities lobby)
NUGEQ	Nuclear Utility Group for Equipment Qualification
NUMARC	Nuclear Management and Resources Council
NUPIC	Nuclear Procurement Issues Council
NUREGs	*Nuclear Regulations* (NRC document)
NURP	Nationwide Urban Runoff Program (of USEPA)
NV	Nevada, none visible
NVLAP	National Voluntary Laboratory Accreditation Program
NW	northwest
NWAPA	Northwest Air Pollution Authority
NWAS	Northwest Aluminum Specialties Company
NWCLF	Northern Wasco County Landfill
NWI	National Wetlands Inventory (map makers)
NWNG	Northwest Natural Gas (a company)
NWPP	Northwest Power Pool
NWPPC	Northwest Power Planning Council northwest region
NWR	National Wildlife Refuge
NWREL	Northwest Regional Educational Laboratory
NWS	National Weather Service (federal agency)

NWSWMD	Northwest Solid Waste Management District (Vermont)
NWWA	National Water Well Association
NY	New York
NYDEC	New York Department of Environmental Conservation
NYDEP	New York Department of Environmental Protection
NYSERDA	New York State Energy Research and Development Authority
O&M	operations and maintenance
o.d.	outside diameter
O_2	oxygen
OAQPS	Office of Air Quality Planning and Standards
OAR	operational assessment review; Oregon Administrative Rule (document section)
OBE	operating-basis earthquake
OCA	overall channel accuracy
OCB	oil circuit breaker
OCC	old corrugated containers; other corrugated containers
OCP	organochlorine pesticide
OCR	Optical Character Recognition
OCS	Outer Continental Shelf
ODBC	Open Database Communication
ODCM	*Offsite Dose Calculation Manual* (document)
ODFW	Oregon Department of Fish and Wildlife
ODOC	Oregon Department of Commerce
ODOE	Oregon Department of Energy
ODOT	Oregon Department of Transportation
OE	operating experience
OEA	Office of Environmental Assessment (of EPA)
OEAS	*Oregon Environmental and Analytical Standard* (document)
OECM	Office of Enforcement and Compliance Monitoring
OECR	Oregon Environmental Cleanup Rule
OERP	operating experience review program
OERR	Office of Emergency and Remedial Response (OSWER)
OEW	ordnance and explosive waste
$^{\circ}F$	degree(s) Fahrenheit
OFM	Oregon fire marshal; Office of Financial Management (Washington state)
OGIS	Open GeoData Interoperability Specification
OH	Ohio
OHSD	Oregon Health Sciences Division
OHSU	Oregon Health Sciences University

OI	operating instruction; oil impregnated
OIRM	Office of Information Resources Management
OK	Oklahoma
OL	overload (adjective, e.g., OL contact); over the line, organic
OLE	Object Linking and Embedding
OMB	outside missile barrier
OMD	Oregon Military Department
OMG	Object Management Group
OMM	operation and maintenance manual
OMS	overpressure-mitigating system; Office of Mobile Sources
OMSI	Oregon Museum of Science and Industry
ONI	off-normal instruction
OOSHC	*Oregon Occupational Safety and Health Code* (document)
OP	operating permit
OPA	Oil Pollution Act of 1990
OPP	organophosphorus pesticide
OPR	operator
OPUS	OnLine Positioning User Service (service of NGS)
OR	Oregon
ORA	orifice rod assembly
ORP	oxidation reduction potential
ORS	Oregon Revised Statute
Ortho-P	orthophosphate-phosphorus
OSC	operations support center; operational support center
OSF	Open Systems Foundation
OSHA	Occupational Safety and Health Administration (federal agency)
OSHD	Oregon State Health Division
OSI	Open Systems Interconnection
OSSC	*Oregon Structural Specialty Code*
OSTF	Ordnance Survey Transfer Format
OSWER	Office of Solid Waste and Emergency Response
OSWRB	Oregon State Water Resources Board
OSY	outside screw and yoke
OTBS	outside the bioshield
OTM	on-site technical monitor
OTSC	onsite technical support center
OU	operable unit
OVA	organic vapor analyzer

OVM	organic vapor monitor; organic vapor meter
OW	organic waste
OWRC	Oregon Water Resources Commission
OWRD	Oregon Water Resources Department
OWS	oily waste separator
oz	use for ounce only in table/graph/equation, if space tight
P	protective (interlock); poise(s) (viscosity measure); perforation; phosphorus
P&ID	piping and instrumentation diagram; process and instrumentation diagram
P.E.	professional engineer
P.G.	professional geologist
p.m.	post meridian (after noon)—do not define in text
Pa	peak test pressure; pascal(s)
PA	preliminary assessment; pulse-to-analog- (adjective, e.g., PA converter); project assistant; Pennsylvania
PA/RD	preliminary assessment/remedial design
PAC	portal access controller; pulse-to-analog converter; political action committee
PAE	protective action evaluator
PAG	*Protective Action Guide* (Federal Radiation Council document)
PAH	polynuclear aromatic hydrocarbon, polycyclic aromatic hydrocarbon
PAN	peroxyacetyl nitrate
PAR	protective action recommendation
PARCC	precision, accuracy, representativeness, comparability, and completeness (of calculations)
PARMS	postaccident radiation monitoring system
PASR	pending, Action Status Report (type of document)
PASS	postaccident sampling system; procurement automated source system
PAT	policy advisory team
Pb	lead
PBB	polybrominated biphenyl
PC	printed circuit; programmable controller; pressure controller; personal computer; protective clothing; polycoated cartons; point of curvature
PCA	precision cleaning agent; power cost adjustment
PCAP	Preliminary Contamination Assessment Plan
PCAR	Preliminary Contamination Assessment Report

PCB	power circuit breaker; polychlorinated biphenyl
PCC	plant configuration chancre
PCCB	power-controlled circuit breaker
PCDD	polychlorinated dibenzodioxin; pentachlorodioxin
PCDF	polychlorinated dibenzofuran
PCE	tetrachloroethane; perchloroethylene or tetrachloroethylene
pcf	pound(s) per cubic foot
PCI	pneumatic circuit indicator
PCM	phase contrast microscopy
PCP	plant control panel; pentachlorophenol
PCT	peak clad temperature
PCV	pressure control valve
PD	project definition
PDCP	positive displacement charging pump
PDP	positive displacement pump
PDS	plant system design
PDWF	peak dry-weather flow
PE	polyethylene
PEA	primary element accuracy
PEC	peripheral entry controller
PEL	permissible exposure limit
PEP	plant engineering, procedure
PEPMS	process and effluent radiation monitoring system
PERM	process and effluent radiation monitor
PERT	program evaluation and research technique
PES	Professional Engineers Society
PET	periodic engineering test; polyethylene terephthalate
PETS	procurement engineering tracking system
PF	power factor
PFD	process flow diagram
PFRP	process to further reduce pathogens
PG&E	Pacific Gas and Electric (California)
PGE	Portland General Electric Company
pH	hydrogen (ion) concentration
PHA	pulse height analysis
PHC	principal hazardous constituent
PHDW	peak-hour dry-weather (adjective)
PHIGS	Programmer Hierarchical Interactive Graphics System
PHWS	peak-hour wet-season (adjective)
Pi	plasticity index
PI	pressure indicator; proportional-integral (adjective);

	public information
PIC	person in charge; pocket ionization chamber; pressure-indicating controller, product of incomplete combustion
PICT	periodic instrumentation and control test
PID	photoionization detector; photon-induced dissociation
PIM	Petroleum Inventory Mangement
PIMS	radiation-monitoring system
PIP	programs in perspective; photoionization period; photoionization potential
PIRS	project information retrieval system
PIS	pressure-indicating switch
PIT	pressure-indicating transmitter
PIV	post-indicator valve
PL	permissible leakage; Public Law
PLC	programmable logic controller
PLL	phase lock loop
PLS	Professional Land Surveyor
PLUB	power-load imbalance; power-load unbalance
PM	preventive maintenance; particulate matter; plus module; plant modification; project manager
PM_{10}	particulate matter less than 10 micrometers in aerodynamic diameter
PMA	process measurement accuracy; polymer-modified asphalt
PMCR	preventive maintenance change request
pmf	probable maximum flood
PMG	permanent monitor generator; permanent magnet generator
PMP	plant modification procedure; probable maximum precipitation
PMW	primary makeup water
PNA	polynuclear aromatic hydrocarbon
PNB	Pacific Northwest Bell
PNI/EA	performance monitoring/event analysis
PNUCC	Pacific Northwest Utility Conference Committee
PO	purchase order
POC	point of contact, particulate organic carbon; particulate organic concentration; precision oscillator crystal; purgeable organic carbon; point of compliance
POHC	principal organic hazardous constituent
POL	petroleum, oil, and lubricants
POM	plant operating manual (type of document)

POR	power-operated relief
PORV	power-operated relief valve
POSIX	Portable Operating System Interface
POSS	plant operator selection system
POT	periodic operating test
POTW	publicly owned treatment works
POW	power operator
PP	polypropolene
ppb	part(s) per billion
PPC	personnel protection committee
ppd	pound(s) per day
PPE	personal protective equipment
ppm	parts per million
ppmv	part(s) per million by volume
ppmvd	part(s) per million by volume, dry
PPP	Public Participation Plan
PPR	plant problem report
PPRC	personnel protection review committee
PQL	practical quantification limit
PQR	procedure qualification record
PR	power range; purchase requisition; pressure recorder; process residue
PRA	probabilistic risk assessment
PRAC	Pre-Placed Remedial Action Contract
PRB	plant review board
PRE	possible reportable event; preliminary risk- evaluation
PRG	preliminary remediation goal
PRM	process radiation monitor
PRMC	process radiation monitor computer
PRO	possible reportable occurrence
PRO/E	possible reportable occurrence/event
PRP	potentially responsible party
PRT	pressurizer relief tank
PRV	pressure-reducing valve
PS	pressure switch; pump station; primary sludge, project station, polystyrene
PS&E	plan specifications and estimate
PSAR	Preliminary Safety Analysis Report (type of document)
PSC	plant setpoint change
PSD	prevention of significant deterioration
PSE	plant systems engineering
PSEL	plant site emission limit

psf	pound(s) per square foot
PSH	phase-separated hydrocarbon
PSI	pollution source inventory, Pollutant Standards Index
psi	pound(s) per square inch
psia	pound(s) per- square inch absolute
psig	pound(s) per square inch gauge
PSP	peer support program; pipe-to-soil potential
PSR	periodic (preliminary) site review
PSRP	physical sciences research paper, process to significantly reduce pathogens
PSSD	plant safety status display
PST	petroleum storage tank
PSU	permanent single unit (adsorber unit)
PSV	pressure safety valve
PT	pressure transmitter; potential transformer; point of tangency
Pt	reduced test pressure
PTFE	polytetrafluoroethylene; Teflon
PTL	pull to lock
PTS	pressurized thermal shock
PU	power unit
PUC	Public Utility Commission (Oregon state agency); Public Utilities Commission (Washington, Hawaii, and California)
PUD	people's utility district; planned unit development; public utility district
PURPA	Public Utilities Regional Policies Act
PVA	polyvinyl alcohol; polyvinyl acetate
PVAC	polyvinyl acetate
PVC	polyvinyl chloride
PWF	present worth factor
PWM	pulse width modulation
PWR	pressurized water reactor
PWSC	peak wet-season capacity
PWST	primary water storage tank
Q	quality factor (electronics); quarterly
QA	quality assurance
QA/QC	quality assurance and quality control
QAE/S	quality assurance engineer/specialist
QAFR	Quality Assurance Finding Report (type of document)
Qal-c	lower coarse-grained zone
Qal-f	upper fine-grained zone

QAO	quality assurance objective
QAP	quality assurance procedure; Quality Assurance Plan
QAPP	Quality Assurance Project Plan
QAS	quality assurance station
QASP	Quality Assurance Sampling Plan
QASR	Quality Assurance Surveillance Report (type of document)
QC	quality control
QCR	Quality Control Report (type of document)
QI	quality inspection
QN	quality notice
QO	quality objective; quality operation
QPA	quality plan for acceptance
QPI	quality performance index
QPR	quarterly progress report
QPTR	quadrant power tilt ratio
QS	quality support
QSL	quality suppliers' list
QVQS	quality vendor qualification supervisor
R	Reynolds number; roentgen; rejected result (presence or absence of constituent cannot be certain)
R&R	remove and replace
R.C.E.	registered civil engineer
R.G.	registered geologist
RA	remedial action; risk assessment; removal action
RACER	Remediation Action Cost Engineering and Requirements (software)
RACM	regulated asbestos-containing material
RACT	reasonable available control technology
RAD	random-access device (computer term); rapid access data
RADAR	Radio Detecting and Ranging
RAGS	*Risk Assessment Guidance under Superfund* (a document)
RAH	recirculation air handler
RAI	remedial action implementation
RAL	recommended action level
RAM	random access memory
RAM	random access memory; regional administrative manager
RAOM	remedial action operation and maintenance
RAP	Remedial Action Plan
RAS	return activated sludge; routine analytical services
RBC	rotating biological contractor; red blood cell

	(erythrocyte); risk-based concentration
RC	responsibility center; resistor-capacitor (adjective, e.g., RC circuit);
rc	well casing radius
RCA	rack calibration accuracy; radiologically controlled area
RCAP	Resource Conservation and Recovery Act Corrective Action Program
RCC	rod cluster control; reactive current compensator (droop circuit)
RCCA	rod control cluster assembly
RCDT	reactor coolant drain tank
RCL	reactor coolant liquid
RCL-PASS	reactor coolant liquid-postaccident sampling, system
RCP	reactor coolant pump
RCPB	reactor coolant pressure boundary
RCRA	Resource Conservation and Recovery Act (NOTE: pronounced "rickrah," not "are cee are aye"; therefore, use a RCRA issue not an RCRA)
RCRIS	Reserve Conservation and Recovery Information System
RCS	reactor coolant system; radar cross section
RCSA	rack comparator setting accuracy
RCSG	radiological control and shielding group
RCU	remote controlled unit
RCW	*Revised Code of Washington* (document)
RD	rack drift; remedial design
RD/IP	Remedial Design and Implementation Plan
RDBMS	Relational Database Management System
RDC	request for design change
RDCO	regional document control officer
RDF	radio direction finder
RDF	refuse-derived fuel
RDII	rainfall-derived infiltration and inflow
RDMG	rod drive motor generator
RDSI	report of disposal site information
RDT	Reactor Development and Technology (NRC division)
Re	radius of effect (in feet)
REA	Rural Electrification Administration (federal agency)
RECIRC	recirculation; recirculate
REG	(field voltage) regulator; reactor engineering group
REL	rescue equipment locker; rate of energy loss; restricted energy loss; recommended exposure limit
REP	Radiological Emergency Plan

RER	Radiological Event Report (type of document)
RERP	Radiological Emergency Response Plan
RESA	Real Estate Site Assessment
RESAR	Reference Safety Analysis Report (type of document)
	Residential /Commercial (zone)
RETS	radiological effluent technical specification
RF	radio frequency
RF	report of failure (also ROF); radio frequency
RFA	RCRA facility assessment
RFB	request for bids
RfC	reference concentration
RfD	calculated oral reference dose; reference dose
RFD	request for determination
RFE	request for evaluation
RFI	radio-frequency interference; RCRA facility investigation
RFI/CMS	RCRA facility investigation/corrective measures study
RFP	Request for Proposal
RFP	request for proposals
RFPD	rural fire protection district
RFQ	request for quotation (qualifications)
RG	regulatory guide (from NRC)
RGWS	radioactive gaseous waste system
RH	relative humidity
RHM	regional health manager; radiation health manager
RHR	residual heat removal
RHRS	residual heat removal system
RHSM	regional health and safety manager
RI	resident inspector (of the NRC); resistor-inductor (adjective, e.g., RI circuit); Rhode Island; remedial investigation
RI/FS	remedial investigation/feasibility study
RI/O	remote input/output
RIB	rapid infiltration basin
RIL	rod insertion limit
RIP	Receiving Inspection Plan
RIR	Receiving Inspection Report (type of document)
RL	reporting limit
RLE	Run Length Encoding
RLR	referee laboratory replicate
RM	radiological manager; river mile(s)
RME	reasonable maximum exposure

rms	root means square(d) (e.g., 120 V rms)
RMZ	regulatory mixing zone
RNA	ribonucleic acid
RNNIS	reactor nonnuclear instrumentation system
RNO	response not obtained
ROD	record of decision
ROF	report of failure (also PF)
ROI	return on investment
ROM	read-only memory
ROV	remotely operated vehicle
ROW	right-of-way
RP	radiation protection
RPC	Remote Procedure Call
RPD	relative percent difference
RPE	radiation protection engineer
RPEC	remote peripheral entry controller
RPM	radiation protection manual (type of document); remedial program manager, regional project manager
rpm	revolution(s) per minute
RPS	reactor protection system
rps	revolution(s) per second
RPV	reactor pressure vessel
RQD	rock quality designation
RR	refinery residual; railroad, resource recovery
RRO	residual range organics (don't add "s" to abbreviation to make plural)
RRS	required response spectrum
RRTF	Reentry and Recovery Task Force (Washington state task- force)
RS	rising steam
RSA	removal site assessment (Reynolds project); remedial site assessment
RSD	Remote Sensor Data
RSIC	reactor shielding information center
RSP	remedial site project
RSS	remote shutdown station
RT	remote terminal
RTCM	Radio Technical Commission for Maritime Services
RTD	resistance temperature detector; resistance temperature detection
RTK	real-time kinematic
RTS	reactor trip system; radioactive tracer survey

RTV	relay trip valve; room temperature vulcanizing (sealant)
RV	reactor vessel
RVDT	rotational variable differential transformer
RVHV	reactor vessel head vent
RVL	reactor vessel level
RVLIS	reactor vessel level indicating system; reactor vessel level instrumentation system
RW	recirculation water
rw	well bore radius (in feet)
RWIP	removal work in progress
RWP	radiation work permit
RWQCB	regional water quality control board
RWST	refueling water storage tank
S	south; siemens; screen; soil; sulfur
S&EE	safety and environmental evaluation
S/S	stabilization and solidification
SACM	Superfund accelerated cleanup method
SAE	Society of Automotive Engineers; site area emergency
SAIC	Science Applications International Corporation; switch action interrupt count
SALP	systematic assessment of licensee performance
SAM	system analysis model
SAP	Sampling and Analysis Plan (type of document)
SAQIL	significant air quality impact level
SAR	Safety Analysis Report; sodium adsorption ratio'; structure-activity relationship
SARA	Superfund Amendments and Reauthorization Act of 1986
SAROAD	storage and retrieval of aerometric data ("and" correct)
SAS	secondary alarm station; special analytical services
SATT	state aquatic toxicity test
SAVE	Society of American Value Engineers
Sb	antimony
SB	Senate Bill, small business
SBA	U.S. Small Business Administration
SBD	small disadvantaged business
SBO	station blackout event
SBRA	Small Business in Rural Area
SBS	static bypass switch
SC	selenium
SC	South Carolina
SCADA	supervisory control and data acquisition

SCC	security control center, status command center; system capacity chore
SCD	system chance description
scfh	standard cubic feet per hour; standard cubic foot per hour
scfm	standard cubic feet per minute; standard cubic foot per minute
SCH	Seismic Category II
SCI	Seismic Category I
SCP	security control point
SCR	silicon-controlled rectifier; selective catalytic reduction
SCS	Soil Conservation Service (of U.S. Department of Agriculture)
SCU	speed control unit
SCUBA	self-contained underwater breathing apparatus
SD	sensor drift; shutdown (noun/adjective); South Dakota; standard deviation
SDC	services during construction; system development char(,e
SDG	sample delivery group; supplemental data gathering
SDL	sample detection limit
SDM	shutdown margin
SDML	Spatial Data Manipulation Language
SDMS	security data management system
SDR	standard dimension ratio
SDRA	sealed double-ring, infiltration
SDRI	scaled double-ring infiltrometer
SDTS	Spatial Data Transfer Standard
SDWA	Safe Drinking Water Act
SEC	significant environmental concern
sec	use for second only in table/graph/equation if space tight
SECM	sample event control module
SEE	safety and environmental evaluation
SEL	selector; select
SEN	significant event notification
SEPA	State Environmental Policy Act
SER	Safety Evaluation Report (type of NRC document); significant event report; sequence event recorder; significant emission rate
SERI	Solar Energy Research Institute
SETAC	Society of Environmental Toxicology and Chemistry
SF	service factor

sf	some companies prefer ft² for square feet
SFO	stipulation and final order
SFP	spent fuel pool
SFPCS	spent fuel pool cooling system
SFR	Supplier Finding Report (type of document)
SG	steam generator
SGA	sand and gravel aquifer
SGBD	steam generator blowdown system
SGFWP	steam generator feedwater pump
SGTR	steam generator tube rupture
SGTS	standby gas treatment system
SGWL	steam generator water level
SGWLC	steam generator water-level control
SGWLCS	steam generator water-level control system
SHF	super high frequency
SHP	Safety and Health Plan (type of document); also see HSP
SHSO	Site Health and Safety Plan
SHWDF	solid hazardous waste derived fuel
Si	silicon
SI	site investigation; site inspection, safety injection
SIC	Standard Industrial Classification
SIF	Standard Interchange Format
SI-IB	substitute house bill
SIL	significant impact level
SIM	selected ion monitoring; selected ion mode
SIN	signal-to-noise ratio
SINES	Spatial Information Enquiry Service
SiO₂	silica dioxide
SIP	State Implementation Plan; site inspection prioritization
SIPP	safety injection pump
SIR	screening information request, structural interface review
SIRS	storeroom inventory reporting system
SIS	safety injection signal
SITE	Superfund Innovation Technology Evaluation
SL	seal; sludge
SLAMS	state and local air monitoring system
SLI	steam line isolation; spent liquor incinerator
SLIS	steam line isolation signal; steam line isolation system
SM	standard method; silty sand
SMACNA	Sheet Metal and Air Conditioning Contractors' National Association
SMAW	shielded metal arc welding

SMCRA	Surface Mining Control and Reclamation Act
SME	summary material evaluation; subject matter expert
SMIG	*Stock Material Issue Guideline* (document)
SMM	subcooling margin monitor
SMP	Strategic Marketing Plan
SMSA	standard metropolitan statistical area
SMW	shallow monitor well
Sn	tin
SNA	Systems Network Architecture
SNARLS	suggested no adverse response levels
SNC	state nuclear control
SNCR	selective noncatalytic reduction
SNG	synthetic natural gas
SO	spurious operation
SO_2	sulfur dioxide
SOC	synthetic organic compound, semivolatile organic compound
SOCMI	synthetic organic manufacturing industry
SOER	significant operating experience review; Significant Operating Event Report (type of document); significant operating experience report (type of document)
SOP	stock ownership plan, standard operating procedure, standard of practice; shaft oil pump
SOQ	statement of qualifications
SOQ	Statement of Qualifications
SOR	system operation review
SOW	scope of work
SP	Spontaneous Potential
SPC	system planning committee
SPCC	spill prevention, containment, and countermeasure; system performance check compounds
SPCCP	Spill Prevention, Control, and Countermeasure Plan
SPCS	steam and power conversion system
SPD	storeroom practices document
SPDMS	safety parameter display and monitoring system
SPDS	safety parameter display system
SPE	sensor pressure effect; service procurement evaluation
SPEER	spare parts equivalency evaluation report; spare parts evaluation equivalency replacement; spare parts repeating, requisition
SPL	spent pot liner; sound pressure level; soil-pore liquid
SPLP	synthetic precipitation leaching procedure (EPA Method

	1312)
SPLT	synthetic precipitation leach test
SPRR	stock purchase repeating requisition
SPS	standard procurement specification
SPST	single-pole single-throw (adjective, e.g., SPST circuit)
SPT	special plant test
SQG	small-quantity generator
SQL	Structured Query Language
SQL/MM	Structured Query Language/MultiMedia
SRG	Standardized Raster Graphic
SRM	standard reference material
SRO	senior reactor operator
SRR	single-source reduction and recycling
SRRE	source recovery (or reduction) and recycling element
SRS	solid radiologic waste system
SRSS	square root of the sum of the squares
SRST	spent resin storage tank
SRT	solids retention time
SRW	solid radiologic waste
SS	shift supervisor; sampling system; selective signaling; safe shutdown (noun); safety system; suspended solids
SSA	Seismological Society of America; sole source aquifer
SSB	substitute senate bill
SSC	System Support Center; superconducting super collider; site safety coordinator
SSCR	store stock change request
SSE	safe shutdown earthquake
SSF	slow sand filter
SSFI	safety system functional inspection
SSFO	supplemental stipulation and final order
SSHP	Site Safety and Health Plan
SSHSP	Site-Specific Health and Safety Plan
SSLPS	solid-state logic protection system
SSO	sanitary sewer overflow
SSP	Site-Specific Plan
SSPS	solid-state protection system
SSQAPP	Site-Specific Quality Assurance Project Plan
SSSA	Soil Science Society of America
STA	shift technical advisor; station; shunt trip attachment
STE	sensor temperature effect; surveillance and test engineering,
STEL	short-term exposure limit

STEP	Standard for the Exchange of Data
STG	stage; steam turbine generator
STLC	soluble threshold limit concentration
STM	steam; system training manual (type of document)
STMP	System Training Management Plan; stamp
STOL	short take-off and landing
STP	sewage treatment plant; sample tracking, program
STS	standard technical specification
STSF	spatial transformation of sound field
SU	startup (noun/adjective)
SV	stop valve
SVE	system valve engineering; soil vapor extraction
SVI	sludge volume index
SVOC	semivolatile organic compound (don't add "s" to SVOC to make plural.)
SW	service water; southwest; switch; surface water
SWAC	Solid Waste Advisory Committee
SWANA	Solid Waste Association of North America
SWAPCA	Southwest Washington Air Pollution Control Authority
SWAT	solid waste assessment test
SWBP	service water booster pump
SWCC	Solid Waste Composting Council
SWD	sidewater depth; solid waste disposal (permit from DEQ)
SWDA	Solid Waste Disposal Act
SWGR	switchgear
SWICSWAB	Southwest Washington Inter-County Solid Waste Advisory Board
SWMG	Strategic Water Management Group (Oregon state agency)
SWMM	Stormwater Watershed Management Model (software)
SWMP	Solid Waste Management Plan
SWMU	solid waste management unit
SWP	service water pump
SWPCP	Storm Water Pollution Control Plan
SWPPP	Storm Water Pollution Prevention Plan
SWS	service water system; security watch supervisor
SWSI	single-width, single-inlet (adjective, e.g., SWSI fan)
SWTR	Surface Water Treatment Rule
SYS	system
T	tera (trillion)
t	ton(s); time since test began (seconds); transmissivity (square feet per second)

TA	trust agreement; teaching assistant
TAC	training advisory committee; toxic air contaminant
TACT	typically achievable control technology
TAFEFU	transfer and fuller's earth filtering unit
TAL	Target Analyte List
TAP	training administrative procedure; toxic air pollutant; tactical action plan
TAPPI	Technical Association of the Pulp and Paper Industry
TAS	thickened activated sludge
TAT	technical advisory team; technical assistance team
T_{avg}	average reactor coolant system temperature
TB	trip blank
TBC	to be considered
TBCW	turbine building cooling water
TBHX	thermal barrier heat exchanger
TBS	turbine bypass system
T_c	reactor coolant system cold leg temperature
TC	thermocouple; to contain (pipette marking); toxicity characteristic
TCA	1,1,1-trichloroethane; time-critical action
TCDD	tetrachlorodibenzodioxin
TCE	trichloroethene; trichloroethane, trichloroethylene
tcf	ton(s) per cubic foot
TCL	Target Compound List
TCLP	toxicity characteristic leaching procedure (USEPA Method 1311)
TCM	transportation control measure
TCP/IP	Transmission Control Protocol/Internet Protocol
TDC	top dead center
TDF	thermal design flow
TDR	time-domain reflectometry
TDS	total dissolved solids
tech	technician
TEDA	triethylenediamine
TEF	toxic equivalency factor
TEFC	totally enclosed, fan-cooled (adjective, e.g., TEFC motor enclosure)
TEGD	technical enforcement guidance document
TEM	transmission electron microscopy
TEMA	Tubular Exchanger Manufacturers Association
TENV	totally enclosed, nonventilated (adjective, e.g., TENV motor enclosure)

TEP	transportation improvement program
TEPS	Total Environmental Protection Support
TER	Training Evaluation Report (type of document); Technical Evaluation Report (type of document)
TERC	Total Environmental Restoration Contract
TFC	thin film composite
TFE	tetrafluorethylene (a plastic)
TFH	total fuel hydrocarbons
TG	top gas
TGL	theoretical ground line
TGOP	turning-gear oil pump
T_h	reactor coolant system hot leg temperature
THM	trihalomethane
TI	technical impracticality
TI	thallium
Ti	titanium
TIC	technical information center, tentatively identified compound
TID	total integrated (radiation) dose
TIE	toxicity identification evaluation
TIG	tungsten-inert gas (kind of welding; see GTAW entry)
TIGER	Topologically Integrated Geocoding and Referencing
TIM	technical interpretive memorandum
TIN	Triangulated Irregular Network
TIR	total indicator reading; total indicator runout
TK	see TNK
TKN	total kjeldahl nitrogen
TLC	ton-layer chromatography
TLD	thermoluminescent dosimeter; total lethal dose
TLV	threshold limit value
TM	Thematic Mapper
TM	temporary modification
TMDL	total maximum daily load
TMP	Traffic Management Plan
TN	Tennessee
TNT	trinitrotoluol
T_o	thermal load under normal operating conditions
TOC	total organic carbon; table of contents; top of casing
TOG	total oil and grease
tonne	1,000 kg
TOP	temporary operating permit
TOS	traffic operations system

TOT	time of travel
TOV	total organic vapors
TP	test pit
TPAH	total polycyclic (or polynuclear) aromatic hydrocarbons
tpd	ton(s) per day
TPH	total petroleum hydrocarbons
TPH-D	total petroleum hydrocarbons for diesel
TPH-G	total petroleum hydrocarbons for gasoline
TPO	term purchase order
TPT	temporary plant test
TQM	total quality management
TR	transformer room
TRE	toxicity reduction evaluation
T_{Ref}	reactor coolant system reference temperature
TRI	toxic release inventory
TRPH	total recoverable petroleum hydrocarbons (don't add "s" to TRPH to make plural)
TRS	test response spectrum; total reduced sulfur
TRTE	time response test equipment
TS	technical specification; total solids (not tertiary sludge; not thickened sludge)
TSC	technical support center
TSCA	Toxic Substances Control Act (1976)
TSD	treatment, storage, and disposal
TSDF	treatment, storage, and disposal facility
TSE	transaction screening evaluation
tsf	transverse shear force
TSI	technical specification improvement; turbine supervisory instrumentation
TSIS	turbine supervisory instrumentation system
TSM	traffic system management
TSP	total suspended particulates; trisodium phosphate
TSR	Training Summary Report (type of document)
TSS	total suspended solids
TTF	test to failure; time to failure; transistor test fixture
TTLC	total threshold limit concentrations
TTO	total toxic organic compounds
TURF	thorium-uranium recycle facility
TWA	time-weighted average
TWAS	thickened waste activated sludge
TWMT	treated-waste monitor tank
TX	Texas

U	undetected at the associated quantification limit
U.S.	United States (use U.S. first definition and no need to define if preceding the noun; note use of periods)
UAA	University of Alaska Anchorage (notice no comma)
UAF	University of Alaska Fairbanks (again, no comma)
UBC	*Uniform Building Code* (document)
UC	undercurrent; upper clay
UCC	Union Carbide Corporation
UCL	upper confidence limit
UEL	upper explosive limit
UF	ultrahigh frequency
UFC	*Uniform Fire Code* (document)
UFSAR	Updated Final Safety Analysis Report
UGB	urban growth boundary
UHF	ultra-high frequency
UHP	ultra-high purity
UIC	uncompensated ionization chamber; underground injection control
UIL	unidentified leak-acre
UJT	unijunction transistor
UL	Underwriters Laboratories, Inc.
ULD	upper-level discriminator
UMC	Uniform Mechanical Code
UPC	Uniform Plumbing Code
UPRR	Union Pacific Railroad Company
UPS	uninterruptible power source; uninterruptible power system; United Parcel Service
URA	urban reserve area (cap only if formal title)
URAL	underexcited reactive ampere limit
URSQ	unreviewed safety question
US	unit substation
USACE	U.S. Army Corps of Engineers (preferred to COE unless client requests COE)
USAEC	U.S. Army Environmental Center (preferred over AEC)
USAED-AK	U.S. Army Engineer District, Alaska (Alaska District); use Alaska District instead of COE or USAED or USACE, for USAED reports (when USAED is the client). Otherwise, use USACE.
USAF	U.S. Air Force
USASI	USA Standards Institute (once ASA)
USATHAMA	U.S. Army Toxic and Hazardous Materials Agency
USB	urban services boundary (cap only if formal title)

USBR	U.S. Bureau of Reclamation
USC	*U.S. Code* (document); unconfined compressive strength
USCG	U.S. Coast Guard
USCGS	U.S. Coast and Geodetic Survey
USCS	Unified Soil Classification System
USDA	U.S. Department of Agriculture
USDI	U.S. Department of the Interior
USDOE	U.S. Department of Energy
USEPA	U.S. Environmental Protection Agency
USFS	U.S. Forest Service
USFWS	U.S. Fish and Wildlife Service (some companies prefer USF&WS)
USG	U.S. Gypsum
USGCRP	U.S. Global Change Research Program
USGS	U.S. Geological Survey
USI	unresolved safety issue
USNAS	U.S. National Academy of Sciences
USNBS	U.S. National Bureau of Standards
USNRC	U.S. Nuclear Regulatory Commission
USPS	U.S. Postal Service
UST	underground storage tank
UT	ultrasonic testing; Utah
UT	Universal Time
UTC	Universal Time Coordinated
UTM	Universal Transverse Mercator
UTS	universal treatment standard
UV	ultraviolet
UV	under-voltage; ultraviolet
UVNIS	ultraviolet/visible
UVTA	undervoltage trip attachment
UW	upper waste
V	volt(s) (e.g., 120-V dc power supply); voltmeter
V&LPMS	vibration and loose parts monitoring system
V&V	verification and validation
v/o	volume percent
VA	volt-ampere; Virginia
VAC	vacuum
VACP	vital area control point
VAS	VISSR Atmospheric Sounder (GOES)
VCH	vent collection header
VCO	voltage-controlled oscillator
VCT	volume control tank

VDT	video display terminal
VEL	vendor evaluation log
VES	vapor extraction system; vertical electrical sounding
VFD	variable frequency drive
VFR	visual flight rule
VGES	variable geometry experimental station
VHF	very high frequency
VHF	Very High Frequency
VI	viscosity index; visual inspection; Virgin Islands
VIRS	Visible Infrared Scanner
VIRSR	Visible Infrared Scanning Radiometer
VIS	Visible
VISSR	Visible/Infrared Spin-Scan Radiometer (GOES)
VLDPE	very low density polyethylene
VLV	valve
VMT	vehicle miles traveled; Valdez Marine Terminal
VOA	volatile organic analytic (via] type); volatile organic analysis
VOC	volatile organic constituent; volatile organic compound
VOCx	halogenated volatile organic compounds
vol	volume
vom	volt-ohm meter; volatile organic monitoring
VOR	very high frequency omni-directional range
VPF	Vector Product Format
VPI	valve position indication
VRF	Vector Relational Format
vs.	spell out versus in text
VSPC	virtual storage personal computing
VSS	volatile suspended solids
VSW	Village Safe Water
VT	visual test; Vermont
VTVM	vacuum-tube voltmeter
VWO	valve wide open
W	watt; west; waste
WA	Washington
WACS	White Alice Communications System
WAG	water-alternating gas
WAIS	Wide Area Information Server
WAN	Wide Area Network
WAP	Waste Analysis Plan (RCRA)
WAS	waste activated sludge
WBD	whole-body dose

WBE	women's business enterprise (designation)
WBZ	water-bearing zone
WC	water column
WDOE	Washington Department of Ecology (use Ecology)
WDR	Waste Discharge Requirements (California)
WDS	waste disposal system
WEF	Water Environment Federation
WET	Waste Extraction Test
WETA	Western Environmental Trade Association
WG	waste gas
WGA	waste generation area
WGC	waste gas compressor
WGDT	waste gas decay tank
WGST	waste gas storage tank; waste gas surge tank-
WHA	wellhead protection area
WHHP	water heater heat pump
WHIP	water heater incentive program
WHP	wellhead protection
WI	work initiator; Wisconsin
WISHA	Washington Industrial Safety & Health Administration
wk	use for week only in table/graph/equation, if space tight
WLA	waste load allocation
WMBE	Women Minority Business Enterprise
WME	warehouse material evaluation
WMMA	Waste Materials Management Act
WMP	Waste Management Plan
WMS	Watershed Management Section
WNWF	wet-weather treatment facility
WOB	woman-owned business
WOSM	woman-owned small business
WP	workplan
WPCF	Water Pollution Control Federation; water pollution control facility
WPCP	water pollution control plant
WPPSS	Washington Public Power Supply System
WPR	work package review
WPS	welding procedure specification; word processing services
WPT	water pretreatment
WQC	water quality criteria
WQPS	water quality protection standard
WR	wide range

WR/R	waste reduction and recycling
WRA	water-reducing admixture; Washington Retail Association
WRC	Water Resources Commission (of Oregon)
WRD	Water Resources Department (Oregon)
WRITE	Waste Reduction Innovative Technology Evaluation (computer software)
WSP	working steam pressure
WSPA	Western States Petroleum Association
wt	spell out weight unless part of combination unit of measure (see
wt/vol	weight per volume
wt/wt	weight ratio (weight per weight)
WTFA	west triangle fill area
WTL	wetland (for instance, WTL3 is a wetland sample designation)
WTP	water treatment plant
WTR	water
WV	West Virginia
WWA	wet weather area
WWTP	wastewater treatment plant
WWW	World Wide Web
WY	Wyoming
XAROUND	cross-around
XCONN	cross-connect
Xe	xenon
XFMR	transformer
XFR	transfer
XPRF	x-ray fluorescence
yd	use for yard only in table/graph/equation, if space tight
Yo	maximum well drawdown in feet
yr	use for year only in table/graph equation, if space tight
Yt	drawdown at time t, in feet
ZID	zone of initial dilution; zone of immediate dilution
Zn	zinc
ZOC	zone of contribution
ZPA	zero period acceleration
Zr	zirconium

14.0 MEASUREMENT ABBREVIATIONS

These are measurement abbreviations many of my clients use. Depending on how often they are used in the text, I might only use them in tables and figures, and spell out in the text; it depends on the word. For example, I always spell out foot or feet and inch or inches in the text, but I do define first use and then use the abbreviation for square feet or cubic feet. This is purely based on number of characters. Since the abbreviation for "feet" is "ft" or at some companies "ft." I don't see the point of using "ft." throughout, which is three characters, when the actual word is only four. Just use your best judgment.

These are measurement abbreviations many of my clients use. Depending on how often they are used in the text, I might only use them in tables and figures, and spell out in the text; it depends on the word. For example, I always spell out foot or feet and inch or inches in the text, but I do define first use and then use the abbreviation for square feet or cubic feet. This is purely based on number of characters. Since the abbreviation for "feet" is "ft" or at some companies "ft." I don't see the point of using "ft." throughout, which is three characters, when the actual word is only four. Just use your best judgment.

A

acre .... ac
acre-foot.. ac-ft
actual cubic feet per minute.. acfm

alternating current... AC
ampere .... A or amp
angstrom ....Å
ante meridiem (before noon) .... a.m.
atmosphere... atm
atomic mass unit..amu
atomic weight ....at wt

B

barrel.. bbl
barrels per day .... bpd
below ground surface.. bgs

board foot .... bd ft
boiling point ....bp
British thermal unit...Btu

C

calorie (small)..cal
calorie (large) ....Cal
centimeter...cm
centipoise..cP
cubic centimeter .... cm^3 (cc for gas volume only)
cubic centimeter-second .... cm^3-sec
cubic foot.. ft^3
cubic feet per day ....cfd or ft^3/day
cubic feet per hour.. cf/h
cubic feet per minute ....cfm or ft^3/min
cubic feet per second .... cfs or ft^3/sec
cubic meter .... m^3
cubic yard ....cy
curie...Ci
cycles per minute..cpm
cycles per second.. cps or Hz

D

decibel .... dB
decibel, A-weighted... dBA
degrees Celsius..°C
degrees Fahrenheit.. °F
degrees Kelvin...K
diameter..diam
direct current... DC

E

electromagnetic force .... emf
electromagnetic unit ....emu
electron volt...eV
et alia (and others) ....et al.
et cetera .... etc.

F

foot .... ft
feet per minute.. fpm or ft/min

feet per second ....fps or ft/sec
foot-pound ....ft-lb

G

gallon ....gal
gallons per acre per day ....gpad
gallons per day...gpd
gallons per minute ....gpm
gallons per second ....gps
grain...gr
gram...g
gram-square centimeter ....g-cm^2
gravitational constant...G

H

hertz...Hz
horsepower .... hp
hour... hr
horizontal to vertical ....H:V

I

id est (that is) ....i.e.
inch .... in.
inside diameter.. I.D.

J

joule..J

K

kelvin (temperature unit) ....K
Kelvin (temperature scale)..K
kilo... k

kilocycles per second (kilohertz)..kHz
kilocalorie..kcal
kiloelectron volt..keV
kilogram.. kg
kilometer... km
kilovolt..kV
kilovolt ampere...kVA
kilowatt..kW
kilowatt-hour ....kWh

L
liter L

M
magnification (power of) .... X (*e.g.*, 5X)
mean lower low water .... MLLW
mean low water .... MLW
mean sea level .... MSL
mega (million) .... M
megahertz .... MHz
megavolt .... MV
megawatt .... MW
melting point .... mp
meter .... m
metric ton .... metric ton or tonne
microgram .... µg
microgram per kilogram .... µg/kg (same as ppb)
microgram per liter .... µg/L (same as ppb)
microliter .... µL
micrometer .... µm
micromho .... µmho
micromolar .... µM or µM
micromoles .... µmol
micron (micrometer) .... µm
microsiemen .... µS
mile .... mi
milliequivalent .... meq
milligram .... mg
milligram per kilogram .... mg/kg (same as ppm)
milligram per liter .... mg/L (same as ppm)
milliliter .... ml (for liquid capacity; for gases, use cc)
millimeter .... mm
millimicron .... mµ
million gallons per day .... mgd
million electron volts .... MeV
million standard cubic feet per day .... mscfd
millivolt .... mv
milliwatt .... mw
minute .... min

molar .... M or $\underline{M}$
molecular weight .... mol wt
mole percent .... mol %
month .... mo.

N
nanocurie .... nCi
normal (concentration) .... N or $\underline{N}$
normal cubic meters .... Nm^3
ounce .... oz
outside diameter .... O.D.

P
page .... p.
pages .... pp.
parts per billion .... ppb
parts per billion by volume .... ppbv
parts per million .... ppm
parts per million by volume .... ppmv
percent .... % (*in tables, spell out in text*)
post meridiem (after noon) .... p.m.
pound .... lb
pounds per cubic foot .... pcf or lb/ft^3
pounds per square foot .... psf or lb/ft^2
pounds per square inch .... psi
pounds per square inch, absolute .... psia
pounds per square inch gauge .... psig

Q
quart .... qt

S
second .... sec or s
specific gravity .... sp gr
square centimeter .... sq cm or cm^2
square feet .... sq ft or ft^2
standard cubic feet per minute .... scfm
standard deviation .... SD
standard error of the mean .... SE

T

temperature (tables only)..temp.

thousand (kilo)...k

ton, metric... metric ton or tonne

tons per day .... tpd

V

versus (tables only).. vs.

volt..V

volume per volume .... v/v

volume percent .... vol%

W

watt..W

watt-hour .... W-hr

week ....wk

weight ....wt

weight per volume..w/v

weight percent .... wt %

Y

yard...yd

year... yr

years before present...ybp

ABOUT THE AUTHOR

Lori Jo Oswald is a freelance technical writer and technical editor who lives in Palmer, Alaska. She received her Ph.D. in English from the University of Oregon in 1994, and later earned a computer science degree. During graduate school, she began her career as a technical writer and editor, and has been writing and editing reports ever since. Additionally, she has taught English and Business Communications at Umpqua Community College, Lane Community College, and the University of Oregon, all in Oregon; Green River Community College in Washington; and the University of Alaska Anchorage. Her businesses include Wordsworth LLC, a technical editing company (wordsworthwriting.net) and Forms in Word (a document design and formatting company). She has also volunteered for humane societies for over 30 years.

Education-based Books by Lori Jo Oswald:

Children's Realistic Animal Fiction of Twentieth-Century North America

Priority on Learning: How School Districts and Schools Are Concentrating Their Scarce Resources on Academics

Quality Work Teams: Rationale and Implementation Guidelines

School-based Management: Rationale and Implementation Guidelines

Style Guide for Architectural, Engineering, Environmental, and Construction Firms

Style Guide for Oil Companies and Contractors